Finding a Job After 50

By
Terry Harty and Karen Kerkstra Harty

D1529432

CAREER PRESS
180 Fifth Avenue
P.O. Box 34
Hawthorne, NJ 07507
1-800-CAREER-1
201-427-0229 (outside U.S.)
FAX: 201-427-2037

FINDING A JOB AFTER 50

ISBN 1-56414-091-1, $10.95

Cover design by The Gottry Communications Group, Inc.

Printed in the U.S.A. by Book-mart Press

To order this title by mail, please include price as noted above, $2.50 handling per order, and $1.00 for each book ordered. Send to: Career Press, Inc., 180 Fifth Ave., P.O. Box 34, Hawthorne, NJ 07507.

Or call toll-free 1-800-CAREER-1 (Canada: 201-427-0229) to order using VISA or MasterCard, or for further information on books from Career Press.

Library of Congress Cataloging-in-Publication Data

Harty, Terry, 1940-
    Finding a job after 50 / by Terry Harty and Karen Kerkstra Harty.
      p.   cm.
    Includes index.
    ISBN 1-56414-091-1 : $10.95
    1. Job hunting. 2. Middle aged persons--Employment. 3. Aged and employment. I. Harty, Karen Kerkstra. II. Title.
HF5382.7.H37   1994
650.14'084'4--dc20   94-3108
                                                              CIP

Acknowledgments

We would like to thank a number of people who have made a special contribution to this book.

To the many men and women who have experienced the "50 and Starting Over" workshop and provided us with valuable feedback as to what worked and what didn't.

To a long list of 50-plus clients who taught us we were all the same—some of us just have a few more gray hairs.

To the Golden Sierra Job Training Agency of Northern California, the Special Services Division of Orange County and the City of Santa Ana for funding the 50-plus program in its infancy stages.

To Tim Duncan, Laura Caccia and the entire NOVA PIC (Sunnyvale, California) for their support.

To Al Saunders of Newcastle Publishing who gave us the encouragement we needed.

Contents

Part 1: Self Assessment

Part Two: Job Discovery

Part Three: Polish and Preparation

Part Four: The Interview

Foreword

During the 1980s, leaving your job became as American as apple pie. Early retirements proliferated as some companies offered huge premiums for employees over 50 to leave. Other firms eased or forced out long-service employees less gently. Many individuals, looking for a change, chose to leave on their own. More will be joining them in the 1990s.

Thus thousands of older Americans are looking for new jobs and careers. And it is a frightening undertaking: Many older job-seekers have neither applied for a new position nor updated their resumes, in years—or decades.

For anyone in this situation, *Finding a Job After 50* offers a realistic, workable solution. This book is a helpful hands-on guide through the worlds of reentry and job-seeking. The Hartys have been there. As your personal guides, they help you think through your own talents and goals and then teach you how to present yourself to potential new employers, re-write your resume and succeed in your job interviews. *Finding a Job After 50* not only helps you land a new job, it makes sure it is the right job for you. The exercises are state-of-the-art, challenging, practical and never boring.

The job market of the '90s is more open to older workers than ever before. Employers are seeking experienced heads and hands, and are no longer looking only inside their companies to fill positions. These changes put older job-seekers in an attractive light. More and more firms are also going to temporary agencies to find skilled managers and professionals. Working at a new company on such an assignment for, say, six months provides new contacts and experiences that may well lead to a full-time position or another temporary assignment.

More openings for older employees are also created by the changing composition of our work force. Young workers are increasingly in short supply; middle-aged workers are more locked into salary needs, family and career commitments. It is older workers who have the most freedom and flexibility— valuable assets that increasing numbers of employers are coming to recognize.

Matching your availability with these employers' needs is the challenge *Finding a Job After 50* was written to meet. Karen and Terry Harty are on your side. They talk tough and straight, where necessary, but are interested first and foremost in teaching you to excel under these new conditions. You couldn't find a better guide.

Paul M. Hirsch, Ph.D.
Kellogg Graduate School of Management
Northwestern University

Let's Get a Few Things Straight

Hold on tight. This workbook can change your life. Continue reading only if you are ready and willing to go to work.

This effort is the result of our experience working with thousands of people, age 50 and over, who sought employment during the past 10 years. Some of these individuals were just toying with the idea of returning to the work force; others were very serious. Although the circumstances that brought them to our seminars varied—forced or elected early retirement, being fired or laid off, entering or reentering the work force after spending years as a homemaker, or wanting to change careers—the situation was the same: All were unemployed.

But enough about them. Why are you looking for a job? Are you a serious job-seeker or just curious about your work options? The self-directed exercises in this book will take you approximately six hours to complete. But you still won't be finished. In fact, this book is just the beginning of an exciting and unusual job search. You'll also need to allot 10 hours for resume preparation and interview practice. At this point you may think, "This is much ado about nothing." It's not.

The four life principles

As corny as it may sound, there are, we believe, four guiding principles to follow as you seek your perfect job.

1. As ye sow, so shall ye reap. Nothing new there. But understand that this biblical quotation has tremendous power if you fully apply its meaning to your job search. The amount of time and focused and thoughtful energy you put into a proactive job search will determine the harvest you will reap. (More on being "proactive" later.) In more analytical terms, let's use the equation $T + E = R$ (Time + Effort = Results).

Research on peak performers, those people who seem to always perform optimally, indicates that one of their differentiating characteristics is they accept full responsibility for all that goes on in their lives. No shirking. No finger-pointing when something goes wrong. They seem to possess an innate and buoyant desire to give themselves completely to a task until they are content with its outcome. With this penchant for accepting responsibility comes the understanding that their lives are fully what they make them.

This is the opposite of a 52-year-old man I know who's still looking for a quick fix. He spends his time and energy tracking down money-making schemes, playing the lottery and applying for jobs totally out of his reach. Seven years ago he bailed out of a stressful job in California's Silicon Valley and has since paid the consequences. During the last five years he held two ill-fated positions, suffered a heart attack, went bankrupt and underwent a damaging audit by the IRS.

Still, he won't take responsibility for the choices he made and continues to pin his destiny on pipe dreams. His wife, once a partner in his plans, left him—not because she no longer loved him, but because she realized his shortcut mentality was affecting her work ethic and values. The last time I saw him he was still playing the lottery, watching "Lifestyles of the Rich and Famous" and feeling sorry for himself.

It's true that in America we've been conditioned to the quick fix and the over-the-counter remedy for our ills and problems. Perhaps the notion began with the Horatio Alger story and became distorted. But as you have undoubtedly discovered, there are no shortcuts to getting the job you want. Like it or not, this job-search effort will require a significant amount of time and energy on your part.

2. You are what you think you are. If you see yourself as basically unemployable, so will potential employers. If you see yourself as someone with a wealth of experience and knowledge who has a lot to contribute to any kind of organization, then *that's* who you are—and how you will be perceived and treated.

One thing we require in our job-search workshops is that the participants dress for work—not for some measly job, but for a job they would give their eyeteeth for. How we dress influences not only the behavior of others but our behavior. When we dress in jeans and tennis shoes, it's hard to conjure up the needed discipline to make job-related phone calls for three hours; our dress tells us to pour another cup of coffee and read the weekly entertainment section one more time.

A study was conducted several years ago to test the validity of the self-fulfilling prophecy. The setting was three different kindergartens. Fifteen children, each with an average I.Q., were singled out by researchers. On the first day of class, each of the kindergarten teachers was told his or her five children were exceptional and great things were expected from them that year. Of course, because the teachers *expected* to see something special in the children, they did. Johnny's letters and Sally's drawings were praised and were always the first ones to go on the bulletin board. At the end of the school year, the researchers told the teachers that, in reality, their "gifted" students had only average I.Q.s. The instructors refused to believe it: In all their years of teaching, they had never seen more gifted children.

Then an even more amazing thing happened: When the 15 youngsters were retested, their I.Q. scores had increased dramatically. What had happened? Simply, the power of expectation. If someone expects (not hopes, not demands, but truly *expects)* a great deal from us, we usually perform as expected, thereby fulfilling our own self-prophecy.

Conversely, if we tell ourselves "I'm too old... I can't do that" or "No one will hire me," we have programmed ourselves for failure. It's been said that our expectations are so powerful, we often rearrange reality just to make our expectations occur. So, you'd better be sure the expectations you have for yourself are high ones.

3. Life is tough. This is a favorite of Terry's. Whenever Karen becomes negative or feels sorry for herself because something has not turned out the way she wanted, Terry announces, in a firm voice, "Life is tough." Now while Terry's comment is not particularly empathetic, it does force one to realize that truly no one promised any of us a rose garden.

Life is tough for everybody. So when you see one of those peak performers sailing through life with a gentle wind to his or her sail, look again. We guarantee such people have experienced—do experience—adversity. How they respond to it will be worth paying attention to. Do they allow adversity to do them in, or do they embrace all parts of life—the bad and the ugly as well as the good? Some of us walk through life like ostriches, hell-bent on putting our heads in the sand whenever something painful or disturbing occurs. But as Marilyn Ferguson explains in her compelling book, *The Aquarian Conspiracy,* pain, conflict and tension are transformations trying to happen. To deny them their transformation is to stifle our personal growth.

Colonel Sanders was 72 when he started Kentucky Fried Chicken. What he had was a recipe for spices and a deep-frying method for chicken he believed was better than anything on the market. He didn't have a 140-page marketing plan to guide him, but he did have an unshakable conviction in the quality of his product. He didn't have the money to set up his own restaurant so he sold fried-chicken operators on the benefits of paying for the privilege of using his recipe. He offered to train fast-food operators without charge. When—and only when—they cooked chicken his way were they to pay him a small royalty. Crazy notion? Most thought so. In fact, Sanders knocked on 964 doors before he got his first "yes." Remember, success only looks easy from the outside.

4. No one is going to rescue you. Not the lottery. Not a knight in shining white armor. Not your family. Not your friends. If you want things to change in your life, you're going to have to do it. An excellent book for women on this subject is Colette Dowling's *The Cinderella Complex.* On the male side of this "take-care-of-me" coin is Dan Kiley's *The Peter Pan Syndrome.*

There is no magic wand. Even if we wanted to, we couldn't make your dreams come true for you. But *you* can. All it takes is perseverance, desire and a commitment to the exercises you're about to take.

Reentry workers often tell us, "I have no idea what I want to do." That makes us nervous. Why? Because they're probably saying the same thing, indirectly, to prospective employers. The truth is: No potential employer wants to sit down with anyone, of any age, and do career counseling. So face facts. What do you want to do? What will someone hire you to do? If you're not sure, don't worry. That is what this book will help you discover.

For starters, make a list of some of the skills, capabilities and experiences you bring to the job market. Skills are *abilities gained through experience.* You may be skilled in working with computers, training others, selling, etc. Capabilities are *things you believe you can/could do if given the opportunity.* For example, you may believe you could be a good instructor because of your knowledge in a given field, your strong communication skills and your organizational ability. Experiences are *things that have given your life meaning and form.* In the spaces that follow, write down five skills, capabilities and experiences you have. (If you have trouble getting started, ask someone who knows you well to help.)

Skills

1. _____
2. _____
3. _____
4. _____
5. _____

Capabilities

1. _____
2. _____
3. _____
4. _____
5. _____

Experiences

1. _____
2. _____
3. _____
4. _____
5. _____

See? You *do* have a lot to offer. So why aren't you working? Maybe it's a poor resume. Maybe your interviewing skills need work. Maybe you're applying for all the wrong jobs. Maybe it's your age. Age discrimination certainly exists. But be careful not to overgeneralize; don't make the mistake of believing all companies prefer young workers. A growing number of organizations actively recruit older workers. And the majority of employers are not deliberately discriminating; they may just be guilty of stereotyping—the psychological tendency to pigeonhole or classify people.

In this book you will learn ways to combat an employer's natural tendency to put you in the "older worker" box. When you begin to proactively counter the negative stereotypes with positive ones, you'll not only feel better about yourself, but your interview batting average will break the .300 mark.

There is one more bonus in this book. Bottom line, if you follow the recommendations in this book, *you should be employed within four to six weeks*. Will it be hard work? Yes, maybe the toughest you've ever experienced. Will is be exhilirating? Yes. Will you feel anxious? Yes. Will you once again feel in charge of your life? Most definitely.

Part One

Self~Assessment

Chapter One

Handling Loss

When you were laid off or fired, you experienced a loss that cut more sharply and much deeper than the loss of a regular paycheck. You lost part of who you were. Right or wrong, America is driven by the work ethic and our self-identity is often wrapped up in our occupation. "What do you do?" is the standard question people ask one another in elevators, at cocktail parties and even at baseball games. Not surprisingly, when our occupational cloak is removed, people of all ages experience a loss of identity and self-worth.

This loss of career identity brings with it loss of purpose, money, power and perks, as well as one of our primary sources for socialization. Maybe you are one of those people who gave yourself to the company—30 or 35 years of loyal service. Now you're unemployed. It's a tough pill to swallow, especially if your heart remains with that organization. So you are experiencing a loss—a loss similar to the death of a loved one or the dissolution of a 35-year marriage. It hurts.

In our own reentry counseling, we have seen firsthand that the field engineer experiences a job loss as deeply as the executive vice president or the supply-office secretary. The pain of job loss cuts across gender and rank. This is because you've invested an enormous amount of time in the venture of work—much more even than in raising your children. For years you've tried to convince yourself it was worth it—worth the extra hours, the ulcers, the headaches, the estrangement from family. Just from the perspective of hours spent, work represents a huge time investment. Once you find your niche, work becomes a vehicle for self-expression and influence—whether on the assembly line or in the boardroom.

But the truth is, you invested something even greater than time in your career. You made a psychological commitment; you wove your days around the belief that what you did counted and that you were vital to the success of the business or operation. That sense of belonging, of being part of something bigger than yourself, represents the real psychological hook of working. In fact, motivation experts regularly confirm that the chief motivator among all workers is "being in on things"—being part of something that matters and believing someone cares what you think. Not surprisingly, when that source of meaning is abruptly taken from you, you're shaken to the very roots of your being.

You also experience a loss of purpose. Work provided structure and purpose to your days. All activities seemed to revolve around work: You got up and got ready for work, spent 8 to 12 hours at work, unwound from work, and sometimes even prepared for the next day's work.

If you are like many people, you're probably amazed at how slowly time goes now. You may have to search for things to do to fill the day.

Well, yesterday was your last day of boredom.

Beginning today, each minute matters and you need to be as energized as you were when you were working. Maybe, even more so! No more afternoon naps. No more goofing off. And especially, no more feeling sorry for yourself. There just isn't time for that!

When we work, our paycheck becomes a given. Once it ceases, we doubt our potency. Why? Because our self-worth is determined in part by how much money we generate, what we can acquire with our money, and what our net worth is. Once the paychecks stop, our self-worth may change. Even if you have accumulated a great amount of money, you may feel uneasy cashing in assets to pay the bills. You may even have calculated down to the day and hour how much longer you can dip into savings before the alarm goes off.

Money (or the lack thereof) makes us all a little crazy. Some people view money as a diminishing commodity: Somehow we're only allotted X amount of dollars for life and once that's gone, well, that's it. If you think rationally about it, this notion is blatantly untrue. There is plenty of money, and we'll always be able to generate more for ourselves. Money is not to be hoarded and fretted over; it's to be used and enjoyed.

In business, money earned is a report card of work performed. Therefore, if for whatever reason we aren't generating any money, we may conclude we aren't worth much. Interestingly enough, even when retirement or a career change is anticipated and planned, seemingly well-adjusted people still find it difficult to deal with the loss of a regular paycheck.

It even happened to Karen's mother. Elizabeth was a successful junior-high-school math teacher for 28 years. Last spring she decided to retire. For years she had accepted retirement as just the next phase of her life. It meant she could come and go as she pleased. She would have time for both travel and her grandchildren. She was in excellent financial and physical health.

Yet retirement has not been an easy adjustment for her. Does she miss her students? A little. Does she miss interacting with other teachers? Hardly at all. Does she miss her monthly paycheck? Absolutely. In her eyes, it validated her self-worth and her contribution to society.

You may also feel your personal power is diminished. The last title you bore carried with it an appropriate degree of power—whether it was overseeing a multimillion-dollar budget and a 200-person department or being accountable to no one but yourself. Organizations are big on levels and titles, which is great for order and flow charts, but such structure can hinder creativity. Yet without a title and assigned functions, you may feel you're tottering on the edge of an abyss. You are, but try not to panic. View the chasm kindly because it represents your unrealized potential. Now is the time to tap into the right side of your brain and play with all the juxtapositions and possibilities that present themselves.

If the company you worked for was an industry leader, you probably enjoyed some prestige and power because of your affiliation with it. You have also probably experienced the rude awakening that jars those who leave such organizations. Where once you were treated with respect, perhaps even deference, now your phone calls are only returned when convenient. Life—in the office, in the school, in the agency, in the government—goes on without you. And without missing a beat. But does that make you powerless?

Actually, you are as powerful as you choose to be. True personal power comes from within; no one can bestow it on you. You may have felt more powerful when you were working, with a paycheck and a busy schedule, but think about it: Perhaps you were living your life to realize someone else's dreams and not your own. Or maybe you were buying into someone else's definition of success. You now have the opportunity to get in touch with your own dreams and make them reality. That sounds like a powerful position.

Finally, the loss of a job can mean the loss of an important vehicle for socialization. Your former colleagues may continue to include you in their gatherings for a while, but the jokes and players have changed. Before long, you may feel like the proverbial fifth wheel. So let it go—all of it. You may need to maintain a professional relationship with your former associates, but—at least for the time being—leave it at that.

So where do you find new sources of friends and support? First of all, if this is a difficult time for you, don't try to establish new friendships. Wait until you are more comfortable with yourself and your new career decision. But do get out with other people and network in a relaxed way. Go to chamber of commerce functions and participate actively in the clubs and societies you belong to. Attend meetings for reentry job-seekers. Contact local support groups. See if any community colleges and/or universities have job-search classes for 50-plus job-seekers. The point is, don't put all your energy into either a new friendship or a romantic relationship right now. You'll need all your focused energy for the job search ahead.

One more word of advice: Remember that no matter how much you need comfort and support, your spouse or significant other did have a full life before your crisis. Don't expect that person to become your *everything*. Go back to Life Principle number 4 in the preface: *No one is going to rescue you.* You have to do it yourself.

The Loss Curve

The following chart identifies the feelings most people experience as they move through the job-loss process. It is not an automatic process, but as you consciously work through your feelings, you will gradually move out of despair and into hope and belief in yourself.

Typically, the *Shock* and *Denial* stage lasts from two to four weeks. It may be marked by deep anxiety, sleeplessness and a loss of appetite. Your world has just been turned upside-down and you feel confused. It may help to talk out your feelings with trusted friends or a caring family member. Eventually, when the phone does not ring, it sinks in that

23

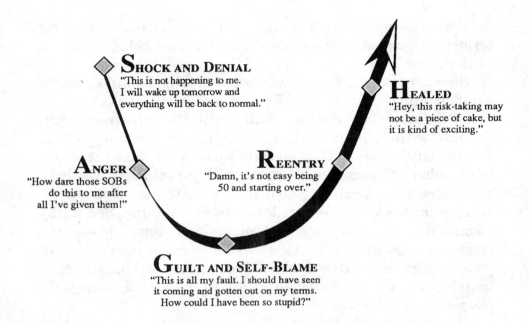

the loss is permanent. With this realization comes *Anger*— but at least this means you have moved to the next stage on the Loss Curve.

You may be surprised at the extent and power of your anger. Yet anger is a healthy and necessary emotion and one you will need to confront head-on. Occasionally, we meet people at our workshops who are still angry, even months after a forced job separation. From their comments we know they are spending lots of energy plotting revenge and reliving certain scenes. Anger is necessary, but at some point it backfires. If you believe the company has robbed you of the best years of your life, then don't give them any more minutes or hours of your time. Don't waste today by fretting about what happened six months ago.

But at least anger is healthier than lethargy. Anger gets the adrenaline going and challenges you to fight back. How long should you be in this stage? It depends on the length of your involvement and the depth of your commitment to the job you lost. Be forewarned, though: After several months, anger can easily turn to bitterness and jade your view of the world. If you become consumed by it, you'll sabotage yourself. Spite will take over, leaving no room for creativity and spontaneity—precisely what you need to start a new life for yourself.

It has been said we utilize only 8 to 10 percent of our brain power or potential. If we expend that 8 to 10 percent on negativism, we cannot make anything good happen for ourselves.

Think of someone you know whose marriage failed. That person either rebounded after a few months or a year or has sunk into an angry and bitter life, blaming his or her former spouse for everything that has gone wrong since the divorce. If you find you are angry most of the time and haven't been able to channel that energy into a creative dimension, it may be time for you to seek professional counseling.

Is there any way to proceed through the Loss Curve more quickly? When you realize your feelings are normal, you'll naturally speed up the process. At least you won't spend any time wondering if you're neurotic. Also, knowing that there is such an animal as a Loss Curve will help you realize that there is life after this ordeal. Beyond that, you just have to give yourself time to heal. It's like the period following surgery: You can be given all the pain pills in the world, but most healing just takes time. Some people say a short vacation is useful. Others rely on family and friends. Eating properly, keeping in good physical shape and getting the necessary sleep will also help give you a better outlook on the world.

The lowest point on the Loss Curve is the *Guilt* and *Self-Blame* stage because here all the negative feelings come to the fore. Yet this stage is a necessary catharsis and a major player in the healing process. Where the prior two stages focused on "them"—what they did to you—the third stage allows you to look inward and see what part you played in the loss. Obviously, it doesn't make sense to accept all the

25

blame; but it is valuable to reassess the situation impartially and learn what you can from it. When you feel strong enough, it is also useful to solicit feedback from those in the organization who saw what really happened. Whatever part you played in the crisis, it's over now. Accept it and learn from it. From this acceptance comes forgiveness. With self-forgiveness comes the potential for true healing and the desire to get on with your life.

Chances are you have already worked through the first three stages and are experiencing the *Reentry* stage (which is why you bought this book). But if you find you are emotionally backpedaling to Shock and Denial, Anger or Guilt and Self-Blame, you may want to let some time elapse before tackling the Reentry stage. If you cannot afford to give yourself the necessary healing time, be gentle with yourself and don't overload yourself with stressful commitments. Take time out for play and be patient. It will get better.

Reentry is fraught with excitement, intrigue, disappointment and risk-taking. It is an exhilarating experience, provided you're ready for it.

The final phase on the Loss Curve is *Healed*. It may be hard to believe now that within several months you will feel stronger than ever and be a wiser and more sensitive person because of your loss. But it will happen. When we speak of this at our workshops, we see lots of skeptical faces, but when it comes together for you, you will feel more accomplished and more in charge than you have in a long time. Will it be worth the loss you've suffered? In retrospect, you'll say, "Yes."

Chapter Two

Taking Risks

Remember when you were 7 or 8 years old and you got the best birthday present of all—a shiny new bicycle? That bike represented freedom: the freedom to escape from your front yard, the freedom that said you weren't a little kid anymore.

But to experience that freedom, you had to take a risk. Learning how to ride that bike meant some banged-up knees and elbows. As a kid you looked that risk in the face, gulped and took it. In the bargain, you acquired a new skill. That new ability brought you the freedom you had before only eyed from a distance.

Oh, to be 8 again! While we probably cannot recapture the same sense of adventure we possessed as children, we can—and should—rethink our views on risk-taking.

When you think about it, every time you try something new or exert yourself in a way you aren't comfortable with, you take a risk. Forging into the unknown can be exciting, rewarding, disappointing, or something in between. Unfortunately, there are no guarantees. But if you reflect on the risks you have taken in your life, you will likely conclude risk-taking pays off. Why? Because, at the very least, you acquired a new understanding or skill from the experience.

Write down three recent risks you took and the payoffs, if any, that resulted.

Risk	Payoff
1. _____	1. _____
2. _____	2. _____
3. _____	3. _____

Were the payoffs worth the risk involved? Even if the result wasn't what you wanted in each case and you had the opportunity to do it again, would you?

If you answered "Yes" each time, great: You have a wonderful spirit of adventure. You understand it's not only results that matter, but also how you play the game and what you learn from it. If you answered "No" to any of the situations above, then this chapter was written just for you!

There are many dimensions to *you*. And only *you* can decide if a particular dimension of your life needs revitalizing through risk-taking. Perhaps you have deliberately structured your life to resemble a pleasant cocoon, and you may be happy with your world. But, in time, cocoons become stifling. When that happens, it's time to stretch the limits of that existence by risk-taking.

Study the Reality Cube in the diagram on the next page. It concerns the patterns, relationships and contents of Karen's life and will give you an example of what it can look like when filled out. These are her issues, her concerns.

On page 30 is a second cube for you to label the patterns, relationships and contents of your life—everything that matters to you. Don't feel intimidated or limited by the number of boxes. If you need more boxes, add them along the sides or on top. If you need fewer, that's all right, too.

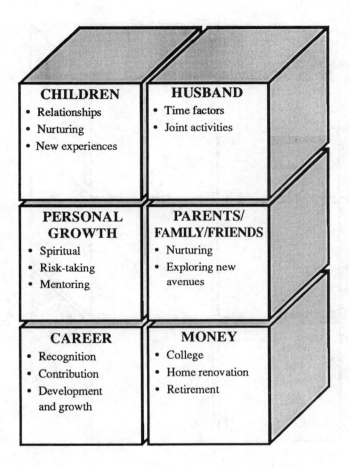

These, then, are the issues and realities you care about. Now take some time to examine what you've written and evaluate as best you can the health of each relationship or issue. Once you've identified your unique realities you can decide which dimensions need stretching.

You may be overwhelmed right now and feel that tackling your career dimension is enough without having to also contend with family, money, kids and other concerns. Hey, you are absolutely right! But life doesn't always work that way. Our personal and professional dimensions will overlap and interconnect whether we like it or not.

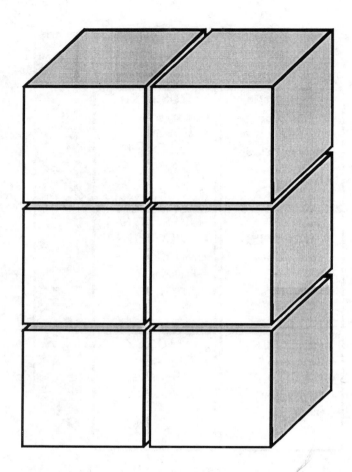

None of us are very successful at separating how we feel about ourselves from how we treat others. We are the sum of the dimensions, issues and relationships that make up our singular reality. What happens at work affects our home relationships and vice-versa. To think otherwise is naive.

Yet, even though we know better, many of us become irritated or overwhelmed when two or more dimensions in our world need attention at the same time. It has been our experience that this watershed experience is almost unavoidable. Why? Because once we take a risk in any single dimension, we alter our view of the world and how the world views us.

Mary is 53 and married to a man 10 years older. They officially retired 10 months ago, leaving their home of 30 years in Southern California to build a dream house on eight wooded acres in California's Sierra foothills. But after the excitement of their new surroundings wore off, Mary's definition of retirement became quite different from her husband's. Whereas George had been a virtual workaholic during their 32 years of marriage, he now was quite content to sit and watch the world pass by. It took Mary days to coax him into town for a simple shopping excursion. Mary became frustrated, bored and lonely. She wanted to travel and explore new interests. Instead, she felt life was passing her by.

So Mary decided to reenter the job market. During her first counseling session she announced she had to "get off that mountain," and getting a job seemed to be the best way to do it. But it soon became apparent that her reentering was really a back-seat issue. More important was learning how to evaluate the different dimensions of her life, setting goals for herself and acquiring better communication tools so she could more effectively deal with the real issue at hand: what she wanted from her life and her marriage.

During our time together, Mary's self-esteem grew; she became quietly assertive and finally was able to communicate her needs to her husband. Eventually, they sold their new house and moved into a medium-sized community. Once Mary resolved her real problem, reentering occurred quickly.

What happened to Mary is a common phenomenon. When job-seekers of any age begin creative job search, they view the world differently. As the job-hunter becomes empowered, a shift in paradigms can occur. It may happen to you.

Another reentry client helped us understand just how much personal and professional dimensions are intertwined. For 25 years Ralph had been a successful restaurateur—four delis and a family-style restaurant. Then he bought another eatery at an upstate location. As Professor Harold Hill tells the townspeople in *The Music Man:* "You gotta know the territory."

Ralph didn't, and the restaurant never got off the ground. Five years later he declared Chapter 11. During this time Ralph worked 50 to 60 hours a week and was rarely home. Had he been asked if he was happy with his life, he probably would have said, "Yes." But when the restaurant closed he finally had the time to assess all the dimensions of his personal reality. During the process he discovered he had nothing in common with his wife. Counseling didn't help. Neither did a trial separation. He is now going through a divorce and is working on a brand-new career.

Has the process been painful for him? Very. Is he unhappy now? No. Actually, it is an exciting time for Ralph. But it wasn't always so. Initially, making job-search phone calls was hard. He was embarrassed by his restaurant failure and, because he hadn't looked for a job in 30 years, was uncomfortable with the entire job-search process. But as he focused on what he wanted and what he could offer, his confidence grew. Together we worked through many of the exercises contained in this manual. Within a short time he secured a sales-management position with a food brokerage company. My last report from him was that he couldn't remember when he'd had so much fun!

Visualize the process of risk-taking as a spiral in motion (see the diagram on the following page). Starting from a position of security (your Comfort Zone), you will gradually move toward Personal Growth—with Risk as the critical link between the two. Each risk taken results in more personal growth. As you become more competent and confident, you reach a new comfort zone—until the "what ifs" of life beckon once again. And so it goes.

You may say, "This is all well and good, but how will I know when a life dimension needs to be challenged or stretched?"

The Risk Spiral

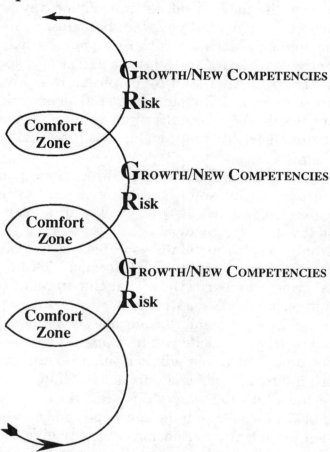

You'll know if you listen to what your heart and head tell you. For example, boredom, anxiety, dullness or a desire to burst out—to grow—will probably motivate you to take a risk. So, too, could the loss of an important relationship.

Someone I know quite well lost his wife after a sudden illness. The pain he felt was sharp. He could have allowed it to eat him up, but instead he went on about his life as best he could. And when he met a lovely lady a few months later, he fell in love. He has been happily married for some time now. Was it risky for him to remarry so soon? Some outsiders may have thought so, but the need to replace his loss and create a new life for himself far outweighed any risk he may have felt. And when *what* you want becomes more real to you than the anxiety associated with risk, you, too, will act.

Sometimes when a person loses a career or a spouse, he or she will try to fill that void by becoming over-involved with other life dimensions. But this doesn't always work. To maintain your psychological equilibrium, you may need to replace the lost dimension or relationship with another of *equal* or *deeper* significance.

Does just the thought of risk-taking make you nervous? Nobody wants to fail and everybody's afraid to. But if you're waiting for that fear to go away, you'll wait a long, long time. Because it will never go away.

The only way to alleviate your fear is to take the risk. Just like with your bicycle. Why? Because risk-taking causes personal growth and growth is what the human experience— yours and ours—is all about.

You are in your comfort zone now, wherever and whatever that is. It is the niche you have made for yourself, and it is comfortable. But if you admit it, it's also, at times, stifling and boring. Or, as someone once said, "Ships in the harbor are safe, but that's not what ships are built for."

It is always easier to hide and hope someone else will resolve your employment situation. But why give someone else the excitement of that discovery? Once you accept the fact that risk-taking is what keeps you growing (and that it offers tangible rewards), you'll never hide from it again.

I often think of a man I met at my first reentry workshop. He had been laid off from his job for three months but hadn't told anyone—not his wife, not his friends, not his adult children. Eventually, of course, his wife found out, but he continued an elaborate charade for his neighbors. Each morning he left the house for a job that no longer existed. He put so much energy into hiding the truth there was none left for picking up the pieces and getting on with his life. Like a turtle, having once been burned by the sunlight, he refused to come out of his shell. The problem is, when you hide you also shut out the possibility of growth and the good things that can happen when you leave your comfort zone.

So go ahead. Right now. Write one thing you know you *should do that will help you get a job.* You know what it is: It's the thing that's been nagging at you, the thing you keep putting out of your mind, the thing that's risky for you. OK, what is it?

_____

_____

_____

Now look that risk in the face. What are the potential payoffs? What do you have to lose? Will it be worth it? Probably. So tomorrow, do it!

Rita Davenport, a time-management trainer, says something we'd like to share with you. She has a wonderful Southern drawl that you'll just have to imagine. What she says is, "Mind your mind." In other words, you have a choice: You can sabotage yourself and live like a turtle, or you can take control of your mind and empower yourself through risk-taking.

The choice you make—to take the risk or not—will affect the direction and outcome of your life. We don't have to be victims in life; fate doesn't beat us up just for the hell of it. We are who we choose to be. Don't give that power to someone else. It is your life. Live it.

Chapter Three

Setting Goals

Now it's time to roll up your sleeves and wrestle with what you want out of life. This chapter asks you to look inward, to identify your values and your roles, and to set realistic personal and professional goals for yourself. Until you have clarified what you are all about—what's important to you, what isn't, what motivates you, what doesn't—you won't be able to present yourself clearly to a potential employer. Remember, the interviewer is not a career counselor. The better prepared you are to answer the inevitable "Tell me about yourself" question you will be asked in your interview (more on that in Chapter 14), the better you will come across and the greater the likelihood you will be offered the job. This requires some serious soul-searching and introspection on your part.

Many of us only grapple with existential concerns when something doesn't turn out right. When the quick fix is not forthcoming and the cosmetic overhaul doesn't work, we turn to introspection and goal-setting as a penance—and a last resort. Unfortunately, when the crisis passes, so often does the soul-search.

In *The 7 Habits of Highly Effective People,* author Steven Covey explains that personal growth doesn't just happen; it's the result of an intense inward search. He says we must start with the inside first: "Private victories supersede public victories."

Covey's message is taken seriously by American business, in part, we believe, because it mirrors Tom Peters' and Robert Waterman's *In Search of Excellence,* which provided business leaders with a radical alternative to numbers-crunching. As management consultants for McKinsey and Company, Peters and Waterman took a firsthand look to see how many, if any, excellent companies were left in America. Their bias, at the beginning of their trek, was that the Japanese had cornered the market on excellence and that American companies were only treading water.

Well, they did find excellence—in large corporations, small businesses and even government agencies. Once they quantified excellence into objective data, they explored the characteristics and qualities of "excellent" firms. Sure enough, they all seemed to march to the same drummer. But instead of structures and rules, Peters and Waterman found champions, loyalty and innovation. Further, they learned that excellent companies had clear missions, a strong understanding of what they were in business for. The key to organizational excellence, they found, was the ability to articulate corporate values and act on them—unconditionally. Remarkably, corporate culture and mission statements became the battle cry of American business leaders in the '80s.

Covey's book takes this notion one step further. He says excellent organizations are made up of effective people. Effective individuals are principle-centered and live their lives based on those precepts.

Role exploration

To help you clarify your values and principles, let's start, as Covey does, with your life roles. In the left-hand column on the following page, list yours—all of them. For example, you may be simultaneously a Spouse, Lover, Parent, Programmer, Reentry Housewife, Friend, Daughter or Son, etc. When you're done, go back over your list and write in the right-hand column the characteristics and qualities you would *like* to possess in each role. For example, under Parent you may want to say: nurture, provide guidance, foster a loving and open relationship with my children, be a role model for honesty, etc. Later you will be asked to translate these "ideal" role characteristics into specific goals.

My roles	How I'd like to be as a:
_____	_____
	_____
	_____
_____	_____
	_____
	_____
_____	_____
	_____
	_____
_____	_____
	_____
	_____
_____	_____
	_____
	_____

Proactive vs. reactive

Initially, you may be uncomfortable with introspection and the demands it makes of you. But in job search (as in anything else), there are two different approaches you can take: proactive and reactive. You can sit in the bleachers and wait for someone else to dole out your life experiences for you, which is decidedly reactive. Or you can actively seek what you want in your life and in your career, which is the proactive approach. The choice is yours. Look at the diagrams below.

Reactive people may be very busy. They may appear overworked and operating in a whirlwind. But activity, even the most frenetic kind, doesn't always produce results. Reactive

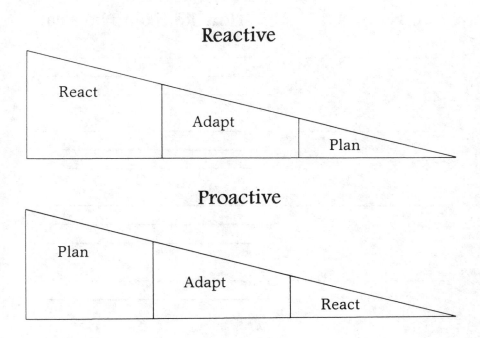

people can be efficient but still not be effective. Why? Because they avoid introspection. They have no idea what makes them tick. Because they never establish goals, they tend to float through life rather than focus on what they want from it. They may jump from one interest and project to another. Things may happen to them, but they rarely make things happen.

As a result, reactive people spend the bulk of their time reacting to their environment, puppets of life's circumstances.

They have no creed, no mission, no plan; on occasion they may adapt to what comes their way, and on very rare occasions they may plan—perhaps for a single event. But they have no *master plan*.

Unfortunately, many of you have probably been "managed" at one time or another by someone like this, a person whose style would best be characterized as "management by crisis." At the end of the day this person will have accumulated a big bucket of sweat. When his boss asks what he accomplished that day, he points proudly to his bucket. But buckets of sweat are no indication that goals have been realized. Our manager is so hell-bent on cracking the whip to produce sweat, it never occurs to him that sweat, in and of itself, is not an accomplishment.

The same thing applies to job-seekers. Instead of first asking, "Who am I and what career makes sense for me?" the reactive job-seeker reads the Sunday want ads—allowing his or her career to be determined by what's in that week's offerings. He or she is totally oblivious to the statistics that show only 21 to 25 percent of all jobs are filled through newspaper classified advertising.

Proactive people, on the other hand, are goal-oriented. The number-one characteristic of peak performers is foresight. Because they want and need to grow, they pursue introspection. They are comfortable with who they are because they *know* who they are. While reactive people live the same day a million times, proactive people view each day as a stepping stone to something greater.

Proactive individuals plan a lot, too. They identify what they want to happen in each life dimension, and they do what's required to make it happen. They spend their time and energy doing what counts—whatever gets them closer to their goals.

Do things always go as planned for proactive people? Of course not. But when setbacks occur, they adapt (and perhaps even react) to the new conditions while never losing sight of what they value and what is important. Is it hard work? Only at first. Actually, it's quite exhilarating to realize you're in charge of your own life, that you're not the victim of life's experiences, that you can create your own reality.

Reflect upon two situations: one in which you were reactive and one in which you were proactive. How did each work out for you? Write your responses in the spaces below.

Reactive situation: _____

Result: _____

Proactive situation: _____

Result: _____

It has been our experience that setting goals makes many people downright uncomfortable. In our job-search workshops we always ask participants to spend some time focusing on their goals. After a minute or two, some people become so uneasy they actually leave the room! For the uninitiated, goal-setting is not unlike going to the dentist: It's definitely the prudent thing to do, but it's not a lot of fun. And that's why most people don't set goals. It requires soul-searching and possibly some discomfort. But will it pay off? A hundredfold.

Americans have a penchant for quick fixes—from Alka-Seltzer to diet pills to tanning booths to facelifts. But after the initial fizz, the ulcer remains, the pounds return, the tan fades, the face sags. Quick fixes only work in the movies. There are no over-the-counter pills for self-enlightenment.

If you want to set yourself apart from the rest of the job-seekers and want to live your life to the fullest, pursue self-knowledge as if your new career depended on it. In fact, it does.

The seven life dimensions

Look at the diagram on the next page, showing the seven dimensions to your life: Work, Family and Friends, Spirituality, Community, Fitness, Growth and Leisure. (If the dimensions in your Reality Cube in Chapter 2 are more relevant, use them.)

Spend some time analyzing each of these dimensions. See if your involvement in each dimension is proactive or reactive. Are you allocating time and energy to your most meaningful dimensions? What sort of payoff are you getting? Can you rearrange your time and activities to guarantee that your goals will be attained?

The Work category involves your career goals; or, if you are between jobs, the goals you have established for job search and career exploration. How much time are you really spending on this (including networking and volunteering)?

The Family and Friends category involves the quality of your relationships with those closest to you. How much time and energy do you spend cultivating these relationships? Just being in the same house with your spouse or family members doesn't qualify as time spent nurturing the relationships. But sharing a movie does; so does writing a letter or hosting a party. Do you want more togetherness or less?

The Spirituality category concerns your relationship with the world and the meaning you derive from that. It can be organized religion or contemplative time walking on the beach. Are you as spiritually developed as you would like to be?

The seven life dimensions

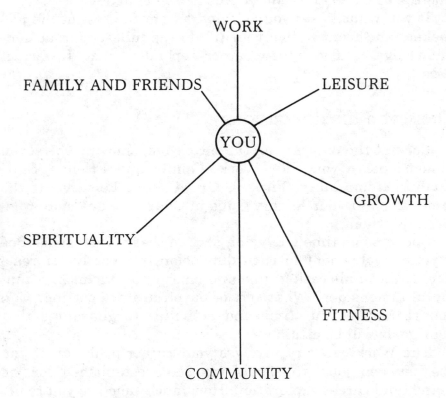

The Community category has to do with how involved you are in your block, your neighborhood, your city in terms of politics, community organizations, volunteer work, etc. Are you pleased with your level of involvement?

The Fitness category is about how much time you devote to keeping your body fit: walking, jogging, tennis, swimming, etc. It also means how well you adhere to a healthy lifestyle: Are you practicing good health habits—eating properly, getting enough sleep and listening to what your body tells you?

The Growth category involves keeping your mind fit. This can mean taking an evening class in computers, learning a foreign language, developing a new interest or hobby, etc.

The final category is Leisure: watching TV, reading the paper, puttering in the garden, going to a ballgame—any activity you do to relax. For many, this category wins hands down as the biggest time expenditure.

In the center of these dimensions is *you*, the manager of your life. Think back on the last seven days. If you slept eight hours a day, you were awake 112 hours last week. How did you spend those hours? How much time did you devote to each of the seven dimensions? Did you watch TV more or less than the national average of seven-plus hours *per day?* Take a few minutes to figure out where your 112 hours went. (Note: Charge household-type chores to the Work category— up to three hours per day, 21 per week. But let's face it, if you're spending more than three hours a day cleaning, gardening or waxing your car, you're doing it because you like it, not because it needs to be done. In that case, charge those extra hours to Leisure.)

All the time you can't account for put under an eighth category labeled Wasted Time or Where the Hell Did It Go?

Dimension	Hours I spent last week
Work	_____
Family and Friends	_____
Spirituality	_____
Community	_____
Fitness	_____
Growth	_____
Leisure	_____
Wasted Time	_____
Total hours:	112

If you're like most people, you will undoubtedly be surprised—mortified is more like it—by the amount of time you spend on Leisure and Wasted Time. You may also be shocked by the paltry amount of time you allocated to job search last week. Since there isn't exactly a line of employers knocking on your door, it would seem prudent to *at least* allocate as much time to job search as to relaxing. We're on a mission here, guys. Let's act like it!

Other than that, there is no right or wrong number of hours that should be spent on any of the dimensions. The only question is whether your time allocations correctly reflect your priorities. "Balanced" people do not necessarily spend an equal number of hours in each of the seven categories, but they do spend their time in a way that reflects their priorities. They are aware of where and how they use their time. They are proactive.

Your life goals

What do you want to happen in each of your life dimensions? The process of identifying what you want to happen is called goal-setting. A goal is defined as a "predetermined idea directed toward a desired result." In other words, it's a target. Set your goal first, and don't get caught up in the particulars. How to accomplish it will become clear later.

There are four criteria to goal-setting.

1. Goals must be written. Otherwise, they're nothing more than daydreams that float away into nothingness.

2. Goals must be specific. The statement "I want a job" is not a goal, it's too vague. "I want a job as an office manager of a 10-person clerical staff in the R&D department of an electronics manufacturing firm" is very specific and far more obtainable. You can see and touch this goal, and it becomes more manageable.

3. Goals must be realistic. If you have two years of college under your belt at age 55, it is probably unrealistic to pursue the goal of being a neurosurgeon.

4. Goals must be assigned a date. If you don't commit yourself to a date, you're just opening the door to procrastination.

Spend the next 30 to 60 minutes working on your life goals. This may prove difficult because you may be unaccustomed to focusing on yourself and what you want out of life. But the first step in presenting a desirable package to potential employers is knowing who you are and what you want.

Under each dimension in the chart on the next page write down a minimum of three goals. Keep telling yourself, "Goals must be written, specific, realistic and assigned a date." You may think you're wasting time by doing this, but you aren't. In fact, *it is the single most constructive thing you can do to begin your job search.*

Work Goals	**Date Assigned**
1. _____	_____
2. _____	_____
3. _____	_____

Family and Friends Goals	**Date Assigned**
1. _____	_____
2. _____	_____
3. _____	_____

Spirituality Goals	**Date Assigned**
1. _____	_____
2. _____	_____
3. _____	_____

Community Goals   **Date Assigned**

1. _____   _____
2. _____   _____
3. _____   _____

Fitness Goals   **Date Assigned**

1. _____   _____
2. _____   _____
3. _____   _____

Growth Goals   **Date Assigned**

1. _____   _____
2. _____   _____
3. _____   _____

Leisure Goals   **Date Assigned**

1. _____   _____
2. _____   _____
3. _____   _____

Congratulations! You are now one step closer to selecting and succeeding in the right career for you. But setting goals is not enough. To meet them, you will probably have to change how you live and spend your time. From this point forward, when you begin any new activity, ask yourself, "Is this bringing me closer to realizing any of my goals?" If it isn't, stop doing it!

Focusing on you

In a few moments we're going to take a close, almost surgical look at your specific work goals, analyzing and itemizing them in detail. But first, to get in the proper frame of mind, answer some general questions about yourself and your future.

Think of goal-setting as a good road map on which you have identified important destinations for all aspects of your life. Answer the questions below candidly and realistically:

1. Where do you want to be in five years? Professionally? Personally?

_____

_____

_____

2. What do you *already* know you must do to realize your professional and personal goals?

_____

_____

_____

3. What risks must you take to reach these goals? Is achievement of the goals worth it?

_____

_____

_____

4. What jobs/careers intrigue you? What qualifications do you have for these occupations? (University and community-college libraries are great resources for career exploration. Large universities have hundreds of trade magazines in the Business Section of their libraries. Also, career centers of community colleges are generally open to the public and have current information on all sorts of occupations and the requirements for them.)

_____

_____

_____

5. What do people always say "you should do"?

_____

_____

_____

6. Aside from educational institutions, who can help you learn about a particular career or trade? To which organization do these people belong? How can you connect with them?

_____

_____

_____

7. Is self-employment a realistic option for you? If so, what type of work could you do?

_____

_____

_____

8. Is temporary employment attractive to you? (Many temporary agencies actively recruit older workers.)

_____

_____

_____

9. What are your immediate career alternatives? Which, if any, are most appealing?

_____

_____

_____

10. What research and planning must you do before you're sure of a successful career path?

_____

_____

_____

11. How do you define success? Is it money? Status? Love of job? Time with family? Something else?

_____

_____

_____

12. How much monthly income do you need to cover basic expenses? Maintain a comfortable lifestyle? Live in luxury?

_____

_____

_____

13. What skills do you have that an employer will buy? What type of employer would be interested?

_____

_____

_____

14. What attitudes do you possess that an employer might buy? Are you energetic? Reliable? Conscientious? Innovative?

_____

_____

_____

15. How far are you willing to drive to work? Would you relocate across town? Across the country? Would you consider relocating if you were offered a position making $100,000 per year?

_____

_____

_____

How to accomplish your goals

Even when our goals are specific and realistic, they may seem too big. So, after you set your goals, break them down into manageable projects. Then break the projects into individual activities. Assign each activity to a given day, then do it. Before you know it, your projects will be complete and your goal will be realized.

Easier said than done, you say. OK, so let's try one example by breaking it down completely—from setting the goal to designating projects to arranging activities. Let's say you no longer want to stay in the career field you've been in for the past 20 years. You are clear about that, but you aren't sure what you do want to do. One appropriate goal for you might be: *By (specific date) I will have explored five new career paths.*

Let's examine this goal in more detail. The first task is to break it down into several projects to clarify what you need to do to. Four appropriate projects might be: 1) Assess your skills, abilities and interests through vocational testing; 2) Determine five careers based on test findings; 3) Conduct primary (talking to those in the industry) and secondary (reading about the industry) research on each of the five careers; and, 4) Network with people in those occupations.

Each of these projects may still seem like a big undertaking to you. So let's break each one down even further into specific activities. Your goal now should look not only obtainable and interesting, but doable.

Goal: Explore five new career paths

PROJECT 1: Assess your skills, abilities and interests through vocational testing.

   Activity 1: Locate testing sources:
      a. Community colleges
      b. Private firms
      c. Call local chapter of American Society for Training and Development for names of reputable consultants who do vocational testing.
   Activity 2: Take battery of tests.

PROJECT 2: Determine five careers based on test findings.

Activity 1: Review and assess test results.

Activity 2: Meet with vocational counselor for input.

Activity 3: Select five careers.

PROJECT 3: Conduct primary and secondary research on each of the five careers.

Activity 1: Identify competent individuals in each career:

    a. Call friends, associates, trade groups to find people to interview.

    b. Set up interviews.

    c. Conduct interviews.

Activity 2: Research industries and occupations:

    a. Locate and read trade magazines.

    b. Check library business indexes to find books and articles about industry in business publications.

PROJECT 4: Network with people in those occupations.

Activity 1: Identify associations for the five careers.

Activity 2: Attend two to three meetings for each career and ask questions about what it means to be a _____.

Setting your goals is an ongoing endeavor. Once you accomplish a specific goal, recognize your achievement and savor the moment—then set a new goal for yourself. Goal-setting is a never-ending process that gives your life direction and purpose.

On the next page is a form to help you organize your goals into projects and your projects into activities. Be sure to make extra copies before you use the original.

Project and activities sheet

Goal: _____
_____

Date Assigned: _____

Project 1: _____

Activities	Date Assigned
_____	_____
_____	_____
_____	_____
_____	_____
_____	_____

Project 2: _____

Activities	Date Assigned
_____	_____
_____	_____
_____	_____
_____	_____

Project 3: _____

Activities	Date Assigned
_____	_____
_____	_____
_____	_____
_____	_____

Now, shoo. Leave this book for at least several days. Do something to get your mind off it for a while. Just let what you've written be for right now.

Welcome back. Now that you've had a decent reprieve, go back and reread all you wrote about yourself and your goals. Pretend you've just come across these papers in the library, left unintentionally by a stranger. Try to make some sense out of this person. What is he/she really like? What are his/her priorities? In what kind of job would this person be most suitable and successful? What do you like—and dislike— about this person? Summarize your thoughts in the space below:

1. What is he/she like?_____
_____
_____
_____
_____

2. What are his/her priorities? _____
_____
_____
_____
_____

3. What job is he/she best suited for? _____
_____
_____
_____
_____

4. What do you like about him/her? _____
_____
_____
_____
_____

5. What do you dislike about him/her?_____

_____

_____

_____

_____

    You may experience two different emotions as you finish this section. You may feel challenged and intrigued by the possibilities that await you. You may also be impatient to learn more specifics so you can make your new career happen. Great. Read on.

Chapter Four

Managing Yourself

Much has been written about time management. But the fact is, we have no influence on time at all. Time is here and it surrounds us. Still, we have always been intrigued with the notion of controlling it.

The point is not how to manage time, an impossible task, but how to manage ourselves within its context. The most powerful deterrent to self-management is assuming we have *forever*. This encourages us to rationalize much of our time (if we don't make that phone call this morning or get the resume out today, it's OK because there's always tomorrow). I call this the Scarlett O'Hara complex. In reality none of us have forever, so if we want to realize our goals, we must get in gear today. This chapter will provide you with some tools for managing yourself so you will be an active participant in life and not a spectator.

If you're like most people, you probably have no idea where your time goes or why so little gets accomplished during the week. Learning to self-manage will require that you look at time in a new way.

There are several idiosyncrasies concerning time. Time is absolutely and totally inelastic. It won't stretch to help you meet a deadline, and it won't shrink to speed you through a trying ordeal. How many times have you taken on too many commitments and would have paid $100 to the gods for just one hour more? But time cannot be bribed. Conversely, no matter how much you want a dull evening to end, it won't until X number of hours have passed.

Time is also perishable. We cannot save or hoard it for when we need more of it. Time just is.

And finally, time is unchanging. No matter how much we may need it, the supply remains constant. Most of us feel we just don't have enough of it.

In addition to these idiosyncrasies, there are a few myths about time.

Myth 1: The harder and longer you work, the more you'll get done. Activity does not guarantee results. Never has. This myth starts early when children are told by parents and teachers that if they "try harder" they will achieve. Trying harder, though, has never been adequately explained.

Myth 2: Those who are the busiest accomplish the most. This relates back to the reactive-proactive discussion. In business, many managers subscribe to the belief "When in doubt, gallop." But if you run from one issue to another, there won't be any time or energy left to set goals, organize projects or arrange activities. Certainly there is no time for introspection.

Similarly, I have seen people latch onto a particular job-search technique as the sole panacea for getting a job. One client of mine, a woman in her mid-30s, once scheduled five networking activities *in one day*. She believed if one was good, three were better, and five would get her a job. But so many commitments forced her to focus all her attention on the logistics of getting from one place to another and on what she was going to wear rather than on what she wanted to gain from the networking. Therefore, she asked no pertinent questions and gathered no leads. At the end of her long day she was exhausted and discouraged—and still jobless.

Myth 3: Efficiency is paramount. True, efficiency counts, but *effectiveness* counts much more. Engaging in the wrong activity efficiently is a waste of time and effort. You may be able to churn out a cover letter and resume on your computer in only five minutes, but if you send them to an organization that's unlikely to need your skills, or to a branch office when they should go to the home office, you have wasted your time. Efficiency experts always start with the desired result, then focus on how to maximize movement and focused energy.

Periodically examine your behavior and activities in light of these myths. You may believe your activities are constructive and proactive when, in fact, they are not—and never have been.

The five steps to managing yourself

How do you self-manage? It sounds like a clever term, but what does it mean? As with everything, it requires rethinking your actions. If you want to devote more time each day to the things that count, effective self-management is a must. There are five specific steps to follow.

Step One: *Identify where time is going.* When you filled out your Seven Life Dimensions back in Chapter 3, you learned in a broad sense how you manage your life—or at least how you spent your time during the last seven days. Now we're going to look even closer at your schedule. Think of yesterday. Reconstruct on the worksheet on page 61 what you did during the 16 hours you were awake. Then look at each activity objectively and determine whether it was worthwhile or not. Did it help you realize your goals?

Most of us waste time the same way every day. If you will study your activity patterns, it will become obvious where and how you waste time. For a more comprehensive picture of how you self-manage, keep a daily activity diary for two weeks and assess your activities in relation to the goals you set in the seven dimensions of your life.

A friend of mine evaluates her activities for the week every Friday and grades each activity with either a plus or a minus. At the end of each month she tallies the score and adjusts her activities to coincide with her values and goals. She holds herself accountable for her life; she is proactive.

Step Two: *Eliminate unproductive activities.* It's as simple as that. Don't do the trivial in place of the significant. Don't walk to the mailbox three times each morning knowing the postman hasn't come yet. Don't spend hours in front of the TV if you don't really enjoy what you see or hear. Don't read the classified section of the newspaper over and over again. Don't allow yourself to waste time. If you spend lots of time worrying and fretting before each difficult job-search phone call, get tough on yourself. Use a three-minute kitchen timer: When the bell rings, make the call. Pretty soon, just looking at the timer will get you going!

Step Three: *Plan each day's activities.* Buy a daily planner, which can be purchased at office products stores and costs from $10 to $150. The fanciest won't necessarily be the best, so look the choices over carefully and select one that best meets your needs. An ideal planner will enable you to plan your daily schedule, keep track of job leads, store important phone numbers and addresses, and record other relevant job-search information. Select one that breaks down each day into half-hour increments. Make sure it has a good supply of daily To-Do lists, which allow you to list every activity you need to accomplish each day. On page 62 is a To-Do list to get you started. Fill it out now for what you plan to do tomorrow.

Yesterday's activities

	Activity	Worthwhile or Not (Y or N)
Morning		
7:30-8:00		
8:00-8:30		
8:30-9:00		
9:00-9:30		
9:30-10:00		
10:00-10:30		
10:30-11:00		
11:00-11:30		
11:30-12:00		
Afternoon		
12:00-12:30		
12:30-1:00		
1:00-1:30		
1:30-2:00		
2:00-2:30		
2:30-3:00		
3:00-3:30		
3:30-4:00		
4:00-4:30		
4:30-5:00		
5:00-5:30		
5:30-6:00		
Evening		
6:00-6:30		
6:30-7:00		
7:00-7:30		
7:30-8:00		
8:00-8:30		
8:30-9:00		
9:00-9:30		
9:30-10:00		

To-Do List

Activity	Priority (A, B or C)
_____	_____
_____	_____
_____	_____
_____	_____
_____	_____
_____	_____
_____	_____
_____	_____
_____	_____
_____	_____
_____	_____
_____	_____
_____	_____
_____	_____
_____	_____
_____	_____
_____	_____
_____	_____
_____	_____

Step Four: *Prioritize your activities.* All activities are not created equal. Some have greater payoffs than others. For example, if getting a job is a top priority, all your To-Do activities related to getting a job need to be prioritized. Why? Because you may have time to do only some of these things each day, so it's imperative to rank, in order, those that count.

One way is the A-B-C method. Categorize those activities that you must do to become employed as "A" priorities. Mark those activities that are important to your job search but not critical as "B" priorities. And check those activities that are pleasant, easy or nonthreatening as "C" priorities.

An "A" activity would be calling back a prospective employer three to four days after an interview. Or following up on a lead you got over the weekend. Or asking a former business associate for referrals—and then calling them. A "B" activity would be scouring *The Wall Street Journal* classified section. A "C" activity would be calling a company's personnel office to see if your resume was received. Look at the activities you marked on the To-Do list on the previous page. Now assign each of them an "A," "B" or "C" priority.

Many people spend the majority of their time doing "C" activities because these fall in their comfort zone. They are safe and require no risk. But if you consistently do your "A" activities first, you will have a better chance of accomplishing your career goals—and on schedule. The Italian economist Vilfredo Pareto first suggested this notion: If we do the correct 20 percent of activities (those with the greatest payoff potential), we will realize 80 percent of our intended results. This is known as the 80-20 Rule. Check your routine tasks and habits and look for the time-wasters—activities that stand in the way of your successful employment. Then eliminate them. Focus your time on what counts.

Step Five: *Arrange your day into blocks.* Research has indicated that it takes one to one and one-half hours to accomplish a thinking task. So look at your To-Do list again and block out a *realistic* chunk of time for each activity. For example, work on one job-search project for at least 90 minutes before moving on to the next one. This will give you enough time to focus and finish each task you undertake.

You've heard this before, but maybe you need to hear it again: No change in the status quo perpetuates the status quo. Change is never easy, but it's the only way to make things happen. Once you begin to manage yourself as you should, you'll be amazed at the exuberance and excitement you will feel. About everything.

Chapter Five

Presenting Yourself

Never have your presentation and communication skills mattered more than right now. To put it bluntly, the decision to hire you has more to do with what happens in a 30- to 60-minute interview than any credentials you might have. Right or wrong, the decision to hire you boils down to the chemistry between you and the interviewer. It's as simple as that.

Many career counselors say that for every $10,000 in salary you want, you must add an additional month to your job search. We don't agree, simply because of the chemistry issue. There's a match or there isn't. It can happen on the first interview or not until the 30th. All we know is that how you present yourself and how you communicate will greatly affect the outcome of your job interview. This chapter will explore both factors.

Normally, when we think of communication we think of conversation. In reality, communication requires more listening than speaking. More specifically, it means *listening for understanding*. For the next four to six weeks listen to what colleagues, friends, vocational counselors, prospective employers and even headhunters tell you about yourself.

The Johari Window

Once you pay close attention and listen to others, you will quickly learn how you are perceived. You may not always be happy with the feedback you get, but that's OK, too. Better to hear it than wander around in ignorance. Learning how others see you is the first step to learning how to effectively present yourself in an interview situation.

Communication doesn't just happen, although we may think it either works or doesn't. We deliberately choose to communicate with someone or not. The model below is the Johari Window, named for its creators, Joseph Ingram and Harry Luft. In

FEEDBACK

EXPOSURE

ARENA	BLIND SPOT
You know something about yourself, and so do I	I know something about you that you don't
FACADE	UNKNOWN
You know something about yourself that I don't	Neither of us knows some things about you

the diagram, the "windows" move to reflect each new situation and how we choose to communicate in that situation.

The top-left window pane is the Arena: In this quadrant *you know something about yourself, and so do I*. The more you choose to reveal about yourself, the more your Arena expands and the more others know about you. The more you withhold information or deceive, the more your Arena shrinks.

To expand the Arena, we must solicit feedback and be willing to expose who we are.

The top-right window pane is the Blind Spot, in which *I know something about you, but you don't*. Many times you're the last to know you've offended someone or have a run in your stocking. The only way you learn is if someone tells you, or you find out yourself. On the flip side, perhaps you aren't aware of how competent, handsome or articulate you are and need someone to spell it out for you.

The bottom-left window pane is the Facade, where *you know something about yourself but I don't*. This represents an upside-down window shade—when we get up in the morning, we pull the shade up as far as our confidence and self-esteem allow us on that particular day. The more you choose to hide who and what you really are, the more your Facade grows and the more your Arena—our only common ground—shrinks.

Which portion of the Johari Window should you expand? No, not the Blind Spot—the Arena. The benefits of an enlarged Arena are several. For starters, you won't have to expend energy pretending all is well when it isn't. Second, when you deliberately deceive others, communication falls apart.

If you handle a business failure or job layoff candidly in an interview and then move on to more positive issues, so, too, will the interviewer. If the interviewer senses something isn't right and doesn't know why, he or she will stay on the sensitive topic.

To expand your Arena (what you know about yourself and what others know about you), you need to do two things: 1) Ask for feedback, and 2) expose more of yourself. If you ask for feedback, your Blind Spot will naturally shrink. You will know how others view you and gain more self-knowledge. As you expose more of yourself to others, your Facade will drop and your Arena will expand.

The bottom-right quadrant is called the Unknown, your untapped potential: *Neither of us knows some things about you.* The only way to tap into your Unknown is to expand your Arena—that which you openly share with others.

In a practical way, the Johari Window can explain the double-edged process of creative job search. By asking for feedback from others ("Can you see me as a _____? Why or why not? What do you see me doing well?"), you reduce your Blind Spot and learn a lot about yourself. Conversely, if during informational interviewing and networking (more on these in Chapter 7) you drop your Facade by letting others know your skills and see your talents—as well as your short-comings—you will learn much. You will become more comfortable with yourself and what you have to offer, and your confidence—and Arena—will grow.

The Johari Window is also useful in understanding the importance of feedback. You get feedback constantly: from your spouse, from your children, from your dog. Often we ignore or deny it. Only by paying attention to all of its many forms, however, can we get a true reading of ourselves and how we come across to others. This may be unnerving if you're unaccustomed to taking feedback seriously, much less soliciting it. But from now on (even after you get the job of your dreams), treat feedback as your friend. Why? Because it will allow you to become more effective in your interaction with others.

For example, if you make 12 phone calls to set up informational interviews and can't find anyone willing to spend just 20 minutes with you, the feedback clearly suggests you have the problem, not *they.* All 12 people can't be busy. You aren't being persuasive, or upbeat, or whatever. Your assignment, then, would be to figure out what that "whatever" is, and correct it.

Communication occurs between two active participants. If your spouse is talking to you and you're tuned out because you've heard it all before, no communication is going on. If a friend tells you she doesn't think your career choice is a good one and you automatically discount her opinion, no communication is going on.

OK, you may say, all this talk about communication and the Johari Window is interesting, but I'm not sure it's all that relevant to job search. Well, it's true the interview is a crazy, unpredictable game and it's often not played fairly, but I've seen more job-seekers succeed among those who present their skills and attitudes openly than among those who attempt to hide issues or inflate their worth.

In the following diagram, Person A sends the message. Person B receives it, thinks about it, and responds with feedback. In real life, however, things interfere with this process. Expectation often plays havoc with communication. For example, if you *expect* not to be offered a job, you probably won't hear positive comments the interviewer drops your way.

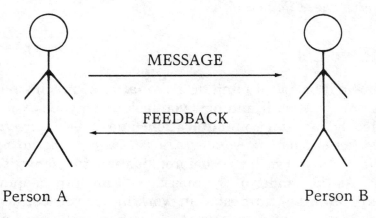

MESSAGE

FEEDBACK

Person A   Person B

Think back on your last interview. (If you haven't been on one yet, or haven't had one in a long time, think of an exchange in which something important was at stake.) What messages did you send? What kind of feedback did you get? A furrowed brow? A phone call taken? A quizzical look? A smile or compliment? All are forms of feedback. How did you react to it? Did you acknowledge it? Ignore it? Assess it? Respond to it?

When communication truly occurs between two people, a synergy results. Did you feel you were really communicating with the interviewer—that he or she really got to know and evaluate you for the person you are—or did the two of you merely go through the motions? Why or why not? Would you do anything differently if you could do it again?

When communication breaks down, we usually blame the other guy. ("That so-and-so.") But in job search, you can't afford to play that game; too much is at stake. Sure, there are plenty of terrible interviewers out there. Some just don't know how to do it, some are uncomfortable asking tough questions, some don't care who you are. The point is, don't let the interviewer stand in the way of your gaining a good career or job opportunity. Do your best to initiate conversation and relax the interviewer. "Not fair!" you may say. "I'm the one who's nervous." We say, review Principle number 3 in the Preface: *Life is tough.*

The three C's

Believe it or not, it often doesn't matter so much what you say as how you say it and how you look when you say it. This is called behavioral communication, and it *will directly influence the outcome of your entire job search, including the interview.* As you've heard before: "It's not the song; it's the singer." As the sender of the message ("I have these qualities and skills and I'm interested in working for you because..."), you need to be sure your verbal and behavioral messages are *clear, credible and consistent.*

The messages you send must be *clear* because you're competing with 10 or more interview applicants for the job. If your message is muddled or confused, you will get lost in the crowd and be dismissed. If your message is vague ("To be honest, I really don't know what I want to do"), you will be discarded for more focused interviewees. To even get a legitimate job interview you have to have been selected from 100 to 200 people. Therefore, it makes no sense whatever to tell a prospective employer you're unsure about reentering the work force!

Clarity from the interviewer's viewpoint also means: Do you look and act the part? If the interviewer expects someone more professional, educated and/or experienced than you are, he or she will undoubtedly be disappointed. But how will you know? From the feedback you're getting. Be alert for this. If you sense the interviewer hoped you would be different, you might say: "I can tell I'm a little different from what you expected. Can you tell me why?" Most likely he or she will tell you. Great! Use that response to your advantage and explain how those differences make you the *best* candidate!

The messages you send must also be *credible*. To be taken seriously, you must be believable. Your credibility will be determined by your self-knowledge, your understanding of the organization, and your technical knowledge and expertise. How you express your sincerity will either enhance or detract from your credibility. Practice talking about yourself in a calm and assured manner and never suggest you know more than you actually do. More often than not, blowing your knowledge out of proportion will backfire.

And lastly, your messages must be *consistent*. That's so when you're called back for a second or third interview, your story and presentation will remain the same. You must look, act and have the same level of energy as in round one.

In our opinion, the three C's explain why fast-food franchises are so successful. When you walk into one of these establishments you have certain expectations that have been raised by millions of dollars worth of advertising. McDonald's sends out clear messages that its food is hot, tasty, fast, fun and cheap. Its *credibility* comes from delivering the goods.

It's *consistent* because every time you walk through the Golden Arches, the french fries, Big Macs and chocolate shakes taste the same. Every time. Every place. *That's* the secret of McDonald's success.

Now, do something brave: Ask someone whose opinion you respect how you come across professionally. This is putting the Johari Window into action; this is real risk-taking. But it's also feedback, which is invaluable as you prepare for the challenge of interviewing.

A word to the wise: If you want honest feedback, you must ask for it. That means never set the other person up. If you say, "I've had a tough time since I lost my job. I never thought it would be this bad. But now I think I've figured out how to use my engineering background in a new way; I want to kick the idea around with you," your friend would have to be made of iron to tell you your idea is a bomb.

So you'll have to be tougher than that. Instead, say, "I've explored several career options, but I'm open to new ideas. You know me well. I value your opinion and *really* want to know *what you think*. What do you think makes sense for me right now?"

Here you have a chance for some honest feedback. In the first example you were clearly just looking for someone to validate your decision. That has its place, of course, but don't confuse it with a request for honest feedback.

Then, once the feedback is given—and this is the most difficult task of all—*accept it*. Do not attempt to defend your position. If it's an unflattering perception, try to understand why the person sees you that way and what you can do about it. If it's a flattering perception, dig further: What could you do to come across even better?

Then *thank the person,* regardless of the type of feedback, and go to work on your behavioral drawing board.

The behavioral messages you send are critical because they will determine whether you are hired. From the employer's perspective, hiring anyone is a risky business. Let's suppose you sound good but can't do the work? Suppose you can't get along with younger people? Suppose you quit after the employer invests several weeks of training in you? Employers often choose the safest candidates just to offset the risk factor. The safest candidates, therefore, are the ones who send clear, credible and consistent messages. Just like McDonald's.

Another thing to remember about the job-selection process: By its very nature it is intrinsically negative—the process is geared to screening people out, not in. The employer has 10 people to see who all basically have the right experience, the right skills. So how does he or she choose the right candidate? Often it's because the chemistry works. As a consequence, the best person for the job may not always get it. This happens all the time. If you were in a management position before, you probably did the same thing when selecting new workers. Now use this understanding to your advantage and plan how to present yourself as a safe, sure bet. The next exercise will give you some pointers on how to do that.

What's your personality type?

Each of us has a predominant personality type. The following test is designed to show (if you don't know already) how you come across to others. It is adapted from a test created by Tony Allesandra, Ph.D., who's based in La Jolla, California.

When you finish it, give the exercise to someone who knows you well and ask him or her to answer the questions about you. This will serve as a cross-check and provide you with valuable feedback.

Your personality profile

Directions: There are 22 responses. Compare each statement in Column 1 with the corresponding statement in Column 2. Circle the letter to the left of the statement that best describes your behavior *most of the time, with most people.* You need to make a choice for every item.

Column 1

R 1. I prefer to deal with numbers rather than people.

R 2. I'm precise and careful.

F 3. I'm a people-person.

R 4. I approach life in an orderly fashion.

R 5. I use few facial expressions when speaking/listening.

R 6. My conversations are task-oriented.

F 7. I express myself well; I'm comfortable sharing feelings.

F 8. I use lots of body and hand movements to express myself.

R 9. I'm less enthusiastic than the average person.

F 10. I'm an intuitive decision-maker.

R 11. I use facts and logic to back up my decisions.

A 12. I welcome change.

A 13. I frequently dominate group discussions.

C 14. I'm easy going.

Column 2

F 1. I prefer to deal with people rather than numbers.

F 2. I'm relaxed and casual.

R 3. I'm reserved and cautious around others.

F 4. I thrive on change and spontaneity.

F 5. I use lots of facial expressions when speaking/listening.

F 6. My conversations include stories and anecdotes.

R 7. I prefer to keep feelings to myself.

R 8. I use few body and hand movements to express myself.

F 9. I'm charismatic and have a sparkling personality.

R 10. I'm a good problem-solver.

F 11. I'm a persuasive communicator who uses ideas and options.

C 12. I avoid change.

C 13. I listen more than I speak.

A 14. I'm hard-driving.

C 15. I'm uncomfortable presenting my cause.

A 16. I'm confrontational.

C 17. I speak softer and slower than average.

C 18. I wait for others to make introductions.

C 19. I don't judge others.

C 20. I dislike power.

A 21. I'm out to win.

A 22. I have a bottom-line approach to life.

A 15. I use verbal advantage to present my cause.

C 16. I present myself in a nonaggressive manner.

A 17. I speak louder and faster than average.

A. 18. I always introduce myself first.

A 19. I believe there are good and bad guys.

A 20. I like power.

C 21. I'll go along so as not to cause a fight.

C 22. I'm supportive and warm.

Add up the number of R's, F's, A's and C's you have. Your R and F scores should total 11; your A and C scores should also total 11. Now you're ready to plot your scores on the Personality Profile Grid on the next page.

Personality profile grid

Mark your scores on the grid on the following page as follows: Find the vertical and horizontal bars (containing numbers from 1 to 11) corresponding to the F, A, R and C categories. Next mark the scores you received in each category by circling the score on the corresponding bars; e.g., if you scored 8 Fs, circle the number 8 on the vertical bar under FRANK (F). Do the same for the vertical bar for RESERVED (R) and the horizontal bars marked CAUTIOUS (C) and ADVENTURESOME (A). Next, connect the four points you have marked. This will produce a kite-shaped form that's uniquely you. The largest area represents your dominant personality.

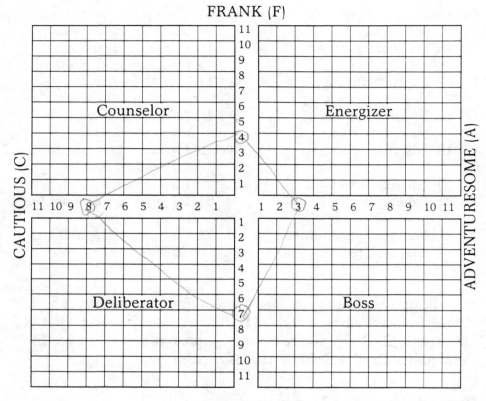

The grid is divided into four quadrants, each one corresponding to a different personality trait. "F" responses mean *Frank*. "Rs" mean *Reserved*. "C" answers represent *Cautious*. "As" translate to *Adventuresome*. To interpret your largest two-area combination, read the following:

If you have a high A score and a high F score: You are the *Energizer*. You tend to be intuitive in your decision-making—data just gets in the way and bogs you down. You are an idea person and like to get everyone stirred up. You do well in front of groups and are a bit of a ham. You tend to generalize and dream, yet you're also a risk-taker. Other Energizer traits: fast-paced, emotional, spontaneous, highly persuasive.

If you have a high A score and a high R score: You are the *Boss*. You don't wear your feelings on your sleeve. You get along well with people but don't like to waste time on what you perceive as needless chit-chat. You're comfortable with power and the trappings that go with it. You have no trouble telling people what to do and how to do it. Other Boss traits: fast-paced, strong-willed, blunt, results-oriented, competitive, decisive.

If you have a high C score and a high R score: You are the *Deliberator*. You like things orderly. You are uncomfortable making decisions. You have a strong need to be right, so you have a penchant for collecting data to back yourself up. You have no problem complying with authority and prefer to work alone. Other Deliberator traits: slow-paced, serious, diplomatic, organized.

If you have a high C score and a high F score: You are the *Counselor*. You are a friendly, supportive person and a great listener. You exhibit open behavior, but avoid decisions because you might hurt someone's feelings. You accept change slowly and are relationship-oriented. Other Counselor traits: slow-paced, cautious, helpful, sharing.

Why should you know about your personality? For several reasons. First, a little insight never hurt anyone. When you are asked that loaded "Tell me about yourself" question in the interview, you will now be able to describe some of the favorable characteristics attributed to your personality style. Second, we all get along best with those who exhibit the same behavior style as we do. Third, it's to your advantage to know, for example, that while the Energizer and the Boss have something in common (strong decision-making tendencies) and the Deliberator and Boss share a common trait (self-contained behavior), the Energizer and Deliberator approach the world very differently. As do the Counselor and Boss.

The Counselor is relationship-oriented. It is important that you know him a little before you get down to business. The Boss is just the opposite: Too much socializing irritates her. She has work to do; why waste time talking about grandkids?

The Energizer, on the other hand, may be an exciting person to be around, but unless and until he settles down and provides you with some hard data somewhere down the line, you can't take him seriously. Because the Deliberator is all numbers and graphs, he sees the Energizer as someone who shoots from the hip. The Deliberator has no respect for intuition; the Energizer prides himself on his gut feeling. And so on.

Think back to a relationship you had with someone (professional or personal) that didn't work out. What are the qualities of the behavior style that's diagonally across from your own? Notice anything?

In business settings people unknowingly surround themselves with artifacts that reflect their personalities. For example, you enter an office filled with plants and flower arrangements. There are pictures of grandchildren and the family cat on the credenza. There is a half-finished cup of coffee on the desk. When you enter, the interviewer shakes your hand and offers you a cup of coffee. In this scenario are you dealing with an Energizer, a Boss, a Deliberator or a Counselor?

Or you walk into an office and see a computer terminal next to the desk. There are few if any papers on the desk, and books are neatly arranged. There are no superfluous objects in the room; efficiency at its best. The interviewer greets you with a firm hand-shake, but does not maintain eye contact.

When he sits down his first comment is, "I have been studying your application and your resume, and I have several questions concerning both." Are you facing an Energizer, Boss, Deliberator or Counselor?

Or you arrive a few minutes early for your 1 p.m. appointment and the interviewer is still out to lunch. She breezes in at 1:10 with an "Oh, I hope you weren't waiting long. Come on in." Her office is disorganized, but there are some interesting art pieces in the room. She glances at your resume, then closes the folder and talks to you candidly about the company and where it's headed. Is this interviewer an Energizer, Boss, Deliberator or Counselor?

Or you're ushered into an office by a secretary who tells you "Mr. Richards will be with you in a moment." There's a big desk in the middle of the office and a leather chair and wall-length credenza behind it. Mr. Richards enters a moment later, shakes your hand and offers you a seat. You sit down and discover he's sitting at a level six inches above you. While he takes a phone call, you survey the room. It is adorned with plaques, awards and diplomas. The desk has an engraved pen and pencil set. Is he an Energizer, Boss, Deliberator or Counselor?

Your answer to Situation One should be Counselor. Why? The interviewer wants to get to know you before starting the interview. That is why you are offered coffee. The plants and family photos are clues that this person is relationship-oriented.

The interviewer in Situation Two is a Deliberator. Everything is organized systematically. He seems more interested in your resume and application than in you as a person. He probably won't make a decision until everything is well-documented.

In Situation Three, you are being interviewed by an Energizer. She's more casual about time, protocol and appearances than the other personality types. Since she tends to make decisions on hunches, she closes the interview folder and tries to get to know you as a person. To her, you're more important than your data. Further, she's candid in describing exactly what the company can and cannot offer. This interviewer sees the hiring process as a two-way street: She wants to know you and wants you to know her—and the company—before a decision is made.

In Situation Four you are dealing with the typical Boss. Clues are all the artifacts in his office that convey power (high chair, big desk and credenza, wall filled with awards). Also, you know he's the Boss by the brisk way he gets down to business.

Human nature being what it is, we tend to feel more comfortable with individuals who seem to reflect our own values, priorities and behavior. It stands to reason, therefore, that the more you can mirror an interviewer's behavior and personality style, the better the chance that the interviewer will "understand" what makes you tick and will like and trust you. When that chemistry happens, you will be offered the position.

In practical terms, though, what does "mirroring" another's personality mean? If you are a Deliberator or a Boss and are being interviewed by an Energizer or a Counselor, try to become more expansive in your responses. Ask the person open-ended questions (ones beginning with who, what, where, why, when and how) that encourage the interviewer to talk. Remember, both Energizers and Counselors love to talk. You can support and acknowledge the interviewer by nodding your head in agreement, smiling, and using your hands to accent what you mean. Quicken the pace of your speech and inject animation through inflection and tone. Maintain eye contact.

Conversely, if you are an Energizer or Counselor and are being interviewed by the Deliberator or Boss, tone yourself down for the interview: Put your hands in your lap and try not to wave them about, lower your voice, slow your speech and speak with deliberation, think before you respond, and state your case in a calm and rational manner.

Is it fair or ethical to present yourself differently from what you really are? We think so. One way to look at it is that you're just being flexible enough to communicate with all types of people. Once you realize the entire job-search process is more of a game than anything else, it's to your advantage to come to the game with a deck that evens the odds.

Chances are you won't be working for the person who interviews you anyway, so why allow his or her personality—or yours—to prejudice the hiring decision? And even if you do work for the interviewer, who says you can't adjust your behavior to some degree?

Sometimes you just have to shake up the chemistry a bit.

Part Two

Job Discovery

Chapter Six

Determining Your Ideal Job

In the first section of this book, you assessed your skills, talents and interests. You also established some important goals for yourself. In this section, you will learn how to analyze your local job marketplace, evaluate your job qualifications, and review your personal job preferences.

Perhaps you've worked for only one organization in your career. Whether it was a small business, a corporation, the government or the military, your job loyalty and security effectively insulated you from the throes, complexities and excitement of looking for work. Until now.

If this is your first time into the job-search waters, you are probably disheartened by the nuances of today's work arena. Already stressed and anxious because you are unemployed, the thought of learning how to find a job—and which one is best for you—can be intimidating and overwhelming. And we sympathize with you.

Almost all those we've met in similar situations have said they would like nothing better than to turn over their career search to someone else. The problem is, that "someone else" doesn't really exist.

Hey, what about headhunters? Or, executive recruiters? They work on commission; they are compensated by the employer for supplying the right candidate for an executive position. Headhunters will actively recruit working executives to fill these positions. Perhaps you got a call or two from an executive recruiter when you were employed. Maybe you even went on an interview. When you are unemployed or reentering the workplace, however, executive recruiters are not very helpful. They're looking for an easy placement and will be able to command more in salary for executives who are employed than for those who aren't. If you go to a recruiter hoping to be represented, do so with your eyes open. This is not to say if an opening comes across his or her desk that matches your experience exactly you won't get a call. You probably will. It's just that recruiters won't go out of their way for "marginal" clients. You, by the way, are considered marginal because you're unemployed.

The exception to this rule are executives who are earning $100,000-plus. Because the potential commission is significant, recruiters will work to place employed and *unemployed* individuals in this salary bracket. Unfortunately, this leaves out many of us! (For more information on headhunters, see the next chapter.)

The second group of job-search professionals that comes to mind are placement agencies that deal with all levels of personnel. For a fee, these agencies will place you with an employer. The fee is paid either by the employer or by you. In either case, it represents a hefty percentage of your first-year earnings. Be wary of committing yourself to one of these outfits. Most placement agencies do little more than send you out for interviews that, with a little legwork, you could have unearthed yourself—and saved yourself up to three months' salary!

And finally, there are career counselors or vocational consultants who will discuss careers with you for a fee. Some charge by the hour ($35 to $75). Others, the high-profile companies with the big display ads in the classified section, will guide you through a job hunt for an upfront fee running into thousands of dollars. And they don't even send you on interviews or have specific jobs to fill. Instead, they give you assessment tests, teach you how to network, and show you the value of informational interviewing techniques you're getting in this book! By the way, career counselors and job-hunt specialists "don't do" placement.

Twelve years ago, when Karen was struggling with career options, she went to a placement agency. The counselor scanned her resume, noted her M.A. in English and teaching experience, then told her she had a secretarial position for her—what was her typing speed? Karen stormed out. Unfortunately, we've heard similar horror stories since then, so we don't think the situation has changed much.

What it boils down to, we're afraid, is you are in charge of your own job search.

At first you may feel like you're stranded in a foreign country where the road signs, laws and mores are vastly different from those you left behind. But, as anyone who has traveled extensively knows, within a week or two you'll feel at home because you'll know your way around. In fact, give it a month and you'll be giving pointers to anyone who will listen!

The Job-Search Triad

So, where to begin? First you'll need to understand the job-search triad. Each part of the triad is equally important and each will determine, or at least influence, the success of your mission. The triad is made up of the *Job Marketplace,* your *Qualifications* and your *Personal Preferences.* Most people focus on the latter two in the mistaken notion that what they bring to the marketplace is what matters most.

The chart on the next page diagrams the Job-Search Triad. Each job variable is represented by a circle. As you can see, each part of the triad is interconnected at one point. And that point where the three circles overlap—where the Job Marketplace, your Qualifications and your Personal Preferences meet—represents your ideal employment opportunity. The more they overlap, the better your outlook for finding a job. If you dismiss any part of the triad as being unimportant you may still get a job, but you won't last long in it. Why? Because it will be a compromise position for you, and ultimately for the employer.

Let's define the terms: The Job Marketplace includes everything that's out there in your community. What's there, in terms of jobs, and what isn't. Qualifications are what you bring to the marketplace: your experience, your interests and talents, your education, your training, etc. Personal Preferences are what you would like from a job: salary, hours, benefits, work environment, commute distance, etc. Let's look at each of these in more detail.

Job Marketplace

To assess your Job Marketplace you'll need to gather the following information about your area: What occupations are in demand? How much do they pay? Which occupations and positions are rarely advertised? What skills, experience and education are needed in what jobs? What is the unemployment rate? What internships or on-the-job training programs are available? How prevalent is age discrimination? (For the latter, see how many ads and industries specifically ask for "recent college graduate.") Buy a large binder and take notes, clip articles and collect data.

The Job-Search Triad

Ideal job = ◭

Where do you get this information? Much of it can be gleaned from the want ads. But don't just look at positions you're interested in; also read other ads to get a feel for the job market *as a whole.* If you have a specific company in mind, monitor it by studying the content and frequency of its classified ads for a few weeks. You should also read the business section of your local newspaper and a local business paper every day, and *The Wall Street Journal* several times a week. It won't happen overnight, but after several weeks of gathering information, you'll have a basic understanding of the Job Marketplace in the area where you want to work.

If you prefer a more documented and scientific approach, you can start with the *Occupation Outlook Handbook,* which is available in the reference section of your local library. This book will give you an industry and occupational overview, plus projections for growth. For local labor-market information, contact the State Employment Development Department and ask for a copy of its *Annual Planning* report. This provides data on labor force, industry trends, occupational outlooks, and social and economic statistics for all regions in your state. Also in the reference section are *Standard and Poor's Industry Surveys* and the *U.S. Industrial Outlook,* both of which describe the past, present and future performance of specific industries and the firms that make up those industries. Other useful reference books are *Encyclopedia of Second Careers, Manual of Professional Career Fields, American Almanac of Jobs and Salaries* and the *Encyclopedia of Careers and Vocational Guidance.*

To focus closer to home, ask the reference librarian for files on local business and area economic trends. Ask to see the *Encyclopedia of Associations* and the *National Trade and Professional Associations of the U.S.* Look up several industries you're exploring and write their trade associations a brief letter requesting industry information. The data are available free or for a nominal fee.

Trade associations are excellent and often overlooked resources for creative job-seekers. If you're lucky, the information you receive may include a membership directory with local names, addresses and phone numbers—certainly an invaluable resource for networking and informational interviewing.

Also ask the librarian for a listing of trade magazines. Read through several in the industry(ies) of your choice. If you want to know about salaries, look in *America's Paychecks: Who Makes What* and the *Area Wage Survey* for your community.

If you want to target the top firms, ask to see *100 Best Companies to Work for in America.*

Mid-level managers often have a difficult time reentering the Job Marketplace because many businesses are downsizing and reengineering the management structure. Often there are lots of entry-level positions available, but the competition for mid-management jobs is fierce. If you're a victim of downsizing and your last position was middle management, you may have a tough time waltzing into something similar to or better than what you left. But there are some ways out of this predicament.

One option would be to go into business for yourself. If your experience and skills are in demand in the marketplace—but not for a hefty salary—consider marketing your services to several different organizations. It can be an attractive solution for an employer: He doesn't have to pay benefits and he can use (therefore pay) you only when he needs you. You win, too, because you get to work and get your foot in the door at the same time. If a full-time opening occurs later, you may get first crack at it. Or you may discover consulting fits you and you no longer want to work full-time for someone else.

Qualifications

Another way to increase your employment opportunities is to update your Qualifications. There are many short-term employment and training opportunities available. Some training programs are funded by the federal and/or state governments and many specifically target older unemployed people. Look in the white pages of your phone book for a Private Industry Council. Ask about vocational and on-the-job-training programs for older workers. Special funds often have been earmarked especially for this purpose. Also call the Senior Community Service Employment Program, the

National Council on Aging, the National Council of Senior Citizens, the National Black Caucus on Aged, and the Office on Aging for back-to-work assistance.

If you don't qualify for federal assistance, consider other training options: High schools offer short-term training through adult-education programs. Some temporary-help agencies will reimburse you for computer or word-processing training that will make you more marketable to their clients. Many community colleges have established reentry programs for both men and women and offer short-term certification programs in all sorts of interesting fields. The fees are minimal, the benefits are great.

Employers look favorably on workers with current training. Not only does it reduce their training costs, but it shows them that you are serious about reentering the work force and understand that to be competitive, you must be well trained.

Personal Preferences

The last circle, Personal Preferences, has to do with everything you want from a job. You will have to decide which are absolutes and which aren't. Obviously, the shorter your laundry list of preferences, the greater your opportunity to find employment.

Some older job-seekers have such a long list that there's no way they'll ever locate an "acceptable" job. We worked with one woman in her mid-50s who refused to even consider work that was *more than five miles* from her home. In addition, she refused to work evenings or weekends! We doubt she will ever find a perfect job—or any job, for that matter.

Now summarize, in the spaces on the next page, what you know, as of this moment, about the three variables. What and where are the good jobs? What do you have to offer? What do you want?

Job Marketplace:

_____
_____
_____
_____
_____
_____

Qualifications:

_____
_____
_____
_____
_____
_____

Personal Preferences:

_____
_____
_____
_____
_____
_____

What you'll probably find is that your Job-Search Triad overlap is small because you haven't investigated the possibilities fully yet: Your understanding of the Job Marketplace is probably limited, your Qualifications may be a bit too generic, and you haven't begun to negotiate trade-offs in terms of your Personal Preferences.

This makes sense. After all, if your three circles overlapped exactly, you wouldn't be reading this book! Your Qualifications would be 100 percent in demand in the marketplace, and your Personal Preferences would be met. It's only when your Qualifications are not in demand in a limited Job Marketplace and your Personal Preferences are unrealistic that problems occur.

Such was the case with Richard, a 57-year-old client of ours who had been personnel manager for a large railroad. When the railroad phased out its local operation he was released—after 30 years with the organization. He couldn't collect his pension money and was too young for Social Security. Because of his experience, it seemed logical, at first, for Richard to try for a personnel-management position with another firm. But he was unsuccessful, and for several reasons. Much of his worth came from his knowledge of the railroad industry. When that industry died, so did his qualifications—and his future career path. Could his training and knowledge have been transferred to a new industry? Yes, but those who interviewed him didn't want to pay him the $50,000 he was accustomed to.

Was this a case of age discrimination? No. In fact, Richard was undoubtedly the preferred choice of every employer he approached. But why should they take him if they could hire someone 20 years younger with specific industry experience who could also do the job? Maybe not as well as Richard could, but the difference wasn't worth an additional $25,000. So, in terms of the Job-Search Triad, Richard's circles didn't overlap or connect *at all*. To get a job, he needed to alter his qualifications and/or his preferences. He rethought his preferences and considered working for $25,000 instead of $50,000, but decided he didn't want to do that. Instead, he chose to alter his qualifications and enter a brand-new career.

I met Richard at that stage, when he was ready to explore new career possibilities. Together we evaluated all his interests and skills in relation to the Job-Search Triad. He wanted a stimulating new career but not a stressful management position where he would have to prove himself every day. He reanalyzed his expense needs in more detail and determined he really did need only $20,000 to $25,000 to live on after all.

After studying his options and interests, we located a short-term training program in commissioned retail sales. The program lasted five weeks, and on the last day of class Richard interviewed with JC Penney. After his first interview, he was offered a full-time position selling men's suits.

Today, after three years in sales, Richard is the number-one menswear salesperson in the district. And the money is fine. Best of all, when he goes home he is able to relax—completely—for the first time in years. No more stress. Within two months, Richard's life had turned totally around. What he did was enlarge his Qualifications with short-term training. By doing so, he discovered a satisfying second career. The same can happen to you.

You can also increase your employment opportunities if you expand your Job Marketplace beyond your immediate vicinity. It stands to reason that if your skills and interests aren't needed in your area, they may be elsewhere. One 75-year-old gentleman we trained enlarged his marketplace to the extreme: He's now setting up a distribution network for a personal-computer manufacturer—in Thailand. In Los Angeles, his age had been a liability, but in the Far East, where the cultures respect age and wisdom, it became an asset.

Only after you expand your Job Marketplace, update your Qualifications and reduce your list of Personal Preferences will you stand a good chance of finding a position suitable for you.

Knowing that, let's return to our Job-Search Triad list and redo it. This time, think how you can creatively enlarge your Job Marketplace, expand your Qualifications, and narrow your list of Personal Preferences. Jot your thoughts in the spaces on the next page.

Enlarge the Job Marketplace: _____

_____

_____

Expand Your Qualifications: _____

_____

_____

_____

Narrow Your Personal Preferences: _____

_____

_____

Now that you've zeroed in on the *type* of job you want, are best qualified for, and can realistically obtain, you're ready to *get* it. To find out how to do that, read the next chapter.

Chapter Seven

Finding the Perfect Job

If you are now chomping at the bit, great. That's just where we want you. It means you're ready to go out and find your perfect job. But how? Where do you start? Where do you look? In this chapter you will learn all about want ads, informational interviewing, networking, profiling, headhunters, temporary agencies, and substituting—all effective avenues for finding your perfect job.

A word to the wise, though: Don't skip any of these avenues just because you think they may not apply to you, or because you've "heard it all before." You may have, but the slant may be different enough to coax forth an idea that hasn't yet occurred to you, an idea that will give you the edge on the competition. Happy hunting.

Want ads

Many job-search books flatly claim that want ads don't produce jobs. Baloney. In fact, that is the beauty of the want ad.

A specific, real-life position does exist and you *can* fill it! I acknowledge that a small percentage of employers occasionally run help-wanted ads simply to see who and what is out there (they have no intention of hiring anyone), but this practice is largely confined to the big guys. And even there, if your response is intriguing enough, you may get a call despite the fact that there isn't a specific job opening.

On the downside, want ads can draw a lot of responses, which can mean tough competition. Depending on the company's name recognition, the economic climate and the position, there may even be an avalanche of responses. Still, answering ads in a professional and intelligent manner will get you some interviews—unless you respond to positions for which you don't qualify. In Chapter 11 you'll learn how to put together a cover letter and resume package that sets you apart from the rest of the pack.

For entry-level sales jobs, clerical and administrative positions the response time to your resume will be relatively short, usually three days but to a maximum of three weeks. It can take three to seven weeks, however, before you hear anything regarding a management position. Keep in mind that this means a *positive* response. If the employer isn't interested, it can take six to 10 weeks before you receive the official "thanks, but no thanks" letter (if the company responds at all).

Therefore, if there is a phone number in the ad, or if you can track down the employer's number yourself, use it first. Talking directly to an employer can eliminate fruitless effort and waiting on your part and will expedite the entire interview process. In the phone conversation, explain your background and qualifications *without emphasizing your age*. Your tone needs to be professional and upbeat. From the conversation you should be able to ascertain if, for whatever reason, you are not appropriate for the position, or if there is the possibility of a match. If your qualifications are on target, your odds of seeing someone within the next few days increase dramatically. In our experience, if all conditions are go, *you can actually get a decent job offer within a day* or two. This, of course, can only happen if you call the employer directly.

Should you be skeptical of an employer who wants to hire immediately? Not necessarily. It could mean one of several things. The need may be desperate: Someone has left with little or no warning and the position must be filled at once. Or the employer may be naive about how to hire someone. Or—the best-case scenario—the employer understands the time-consuming hiring ritual (asking for resumes, screening resumes, setting up interviews, conducting interviews, scheduling second and third interviews, and conducting them) and decides to buck the system. This individual wants to make things happen quickly. God bless him; he could be your next employer!

If the ad requests a resume and cover letter, however, and you cannot call the employer directly, wait four to five days before mailing yours in. Most job-seekers respond to ads when they first see them, which means a whole batch of resumes will arrive on the same day. By holding back a little while, yours will stand apart from the rest and will receive more attention.

What should you do if the ad requests salary history? Ignore it. Or camouflage your answer with vague generalities. The same holds true for salary requirements. True, by ignoring the employer's specific request you run the risk of being screened out, it's a chance you should take. You'll be screened out many more times if you do include your salary history or requirements than if you leave them out. Either you'll be viewed as "too expensive" or "not good enough."

One final comment on want ads: If the ad sounds too good to be true, it is. If the ad is predominantly hype and gives you no clue as to the industry or type of business, be cautious. It might be worth a phone call, but don't waste your time on a resume and cover letter. On the other hand, if an ad is well-stated and provides detailed information but doesn't indicate the name of the company, it could be a winner. Better firms often practice this policy because they don't want the competition to know their personnel needs. Or they may not want an incumbent employee to know his or her future with the company is short-lived.

Informational interviewing

This is a relatively new job-search technique that has yielded excellent results for those who use it wisely. It is simply requesting information about a position or an industry from someone in the know. It could be someone who is in the position to hire you, or it could be someone who has the type of position you want—or think you might want. You're on much more comparable footing in the informational interview because, after all, you're not asking for or seeking a job (not literally, anyway). You're just requesting information. In an informational interview you can obtain current data about career options, information you can't find in industry publications or from outdated books. You are in control of the interview because you decide which questions to ask.

Why would someone in business give you a half-hour of his or her time? For several reasons. Basically, most people like talking about what they do. It's flattering. And it's good public relations. We frequently get requests from individuals currently employed by large firms wanting to know what the waters are like as an independent consultant—and we always end up spending an hour or so with them!

Who should you contact? Keep your eyes open for press releases and articles in local papers, especially business publications. Ask associations, friends and family members if they know someone in your field of interest. Your local chamber of commerce may also be an excellent source. Talk to chamber staff people and ask them for names of knowledgeable people in your field(s) of choice. They have a good grasp of who's doing what and who's good at it. Also, most professional occupations have societies or associations. Call them and ask for names of members who are recognized as the best in their field. The point is, don't hang back and procrastinate; be aggressive ("no guts, no glory").

In the space below, jot down names of five people you could contact. If you don't know anyone in your desired field, write down who you know who *would* know.

1. _____
2. _____
3. _____
4. _____
5. _____

How do you arrange an informational interview? Call the person and explain what you want (get to the point: no hemming and hawing):

*"My name is _____ and your name was given to me by
_____. I am considering a career change from _____ to
_____. I've heard from more than one person that
you are someone I should talk to. May I have 20 minutes of your time to learn more about what it means to
be a _____?"*

If the person says he or she hasn't the time, ask if he or she knows of someone who has.

What should you find out during the interview? For starters, ask:

1. How did you get into this line of work?
2. What is most rewarding about what you do?

3. What is least rewarding about what you do?
4. What does your organization look for when it hires
   a _____ ?

These questions will get you started. Pay close attention to the answers, and ask additional questions based on them. Salary and compensation issues are sensitive matters for most people, so don't ask what the person earns. If the interview goes well, the person may volunteer this information; if not, you can guesstimate based on the office size and decor and the responsibility and power the person appears to wield in the organization.

Be aware of time so you don't overstay your welcome. If the person opens up, feel free to ask if there is someone he or she knows who could provide further insight into this occupation.

After the interview, evaluate what you learned by recording your insights on the Informational Interview Summary sheet on the next page. Make several copies of the form first so you'll have one for each interview you conduct.

Always send a thank-you note to the person you interviewed afterward. It should be hand-written, on quality white notepaper. Two or three sentences should suffice:

"Thank you for your time yesterday. I appreciated your candor. The information you shared provided me with some real insight. Sincerely,"

Many people receive a job offer as a result of informational interviews. So be organized in your questioning, dress for success, present yourself well—and see what happens!

Networking

Networking doesn't just happen. (Nothing really does, does it?) Successful networking means allowing enough time

Informational Interview Summary

Name of person interviewed: _____

Business or occupation: _____

Title or position: _____

Address: _____
_____

City and zip code: _____

Phone number: _____

How contact was established: _____
_____

Date of interview: _____

Positive things I learned from this interview: _____
_____
_____

Not-so-positive things I learned from this interview: ____
_____
_____

Helpfulness of the person I interviewed:

1	2	3	4	5
No help	Some help	Helpful	Very helpful	Great

Does what I learned fit in with my goals, interests, capabilities, education and values? _____
_____
_____

What additional information do I need? Whom else can I contact?
_____
_____
_____

What is my next step? _____
_____
_____

for trust to develop between you and a potential referral source. It means showing up at the same weekly or monthly meetings over and over again. Madison Avenue knows that consumers must view a message six times before the message sinks in. The same holds true for networking. The first time you attend one of these meetings, no one will pay much attention to you. Don't let that bother you; expect it. Smile and introduce yourself, without being pushy. At this point it will do you no good to announce you're looking for a job. No one knows you yet and, trust me, no one particularly cares!

If someone asks what you do, talk about your last position and say you're taking some time off to explore new career options. Show interest in what others have to say and take mental notes. Unfortunately, the second and even the third time you attend these functions, the results won't be much better. But stick to it. Remember: *Life is tough.*

To ease this awkward and seemingly unproductive period, find out who the organization's officers are and approach them. Most groups have hospitality committees to welcome new members. If so, link up with someone else who's new. (Whoever said networking's easy was wrong. But that doesn't mean it can't and won't pay off.)

At your fourth or fifth meeting people may finally start to recognize you and even initiate conversation. Now, when asked, mention you are looking for new career opportunities. At this point someone may give you a name or two to contact and tell you to "use my name." Now the payoff begins!

Since 38 to 43 percent of all jobs are filled by employee or associate referrals, the name you just got is worth its weight in gold. Call the person and tell him or her you had lunch with so-and-so and he suggested you call. You will be treated with courtesy, and if you project your qualifications well on the phone, you may even be asked in for an interview. If the person is polite but tells you a position doesn't exist, ask for an informational interview instead. If the person won't buy that, ask if he or she knows who's hiring in the industry. Again, don't be afraid to push.

Networking can be worth it, but don't expect overnight success. What organizations should you join? That depends on what you want to do. Ask people in specific fields what their professional or trade associations or societies are. At the very minimum, women should attend chamber of commerce mixers and join a women's business network of some kind. All major cities have women's organizations that have formed in the last 10 to 15 years for the express purpose of business networking. Rotary and Lions Clubs are good sources for men, but they may be a little expensive if you're unemployed.

Another networking tactic is volunteering. It can be at the zoo, a hospital, a school, a city or county board or commission, etc. In addition, your local paper probably has a weekly "Community Bulletin Board" listing organizations that need volunteers. Again, don't expect immediate results, but volunteering can be an excellent way to job-network. And besides, you'll be giving back to your community.

Profiling

In your last job you may have connected with vendors, as well as distributors, service representatives, competitors, maybe even CEOs—all sorts of people in a variety of positions. Profiling is a term we've coined for reconnecting with the people you knew professionally, people you liked and people who liked and respected you. Your assignment is to profile yourself to these people in such a way that they will want to interview you for their organization or be happy to refer you elsewhere.

How does profiling differ from networking? Networking involves meeting new people through others. Profiling involves seeing people you already know and with whom you have developed a professional relationship. Your objective is to profile yourself as a potential colleague, one they would be pleased to have on board their own ship.

You can profile yourself in one of two ways. You can call people directly, telling them you are no longer with XYZ Corporation and want to keep them up to date on what you're doing. This should draw inquiries as to what you are doing. To which you respond: "Actually, Bob, one of the reasons I'm calling is that I like how you run your department/business/organization and wonder what opportunities may exist there."

Or you can send a letter stating the same thing: You enjoyed the relationship you shared before, want the person to know what you're doing and think you possess skills that could be applied in his or her organization. Simple letters usually suffice; if people are interested, they'll call. If you wish, you can include your resume. This will show you mean business, but either strategy can work. Obviously, much of the success in profiling depends on the relationships you developed over the years.

This technique can work well, but—and I can't emphasize this enough—you must take the initiative. It won't be enough to simply say you are no longer working for XYZ Corporation and then cross your fingers, hoping they'll get the hint and invite you in to a meeting or an interview. Your former associates have probably never thought of you in that context. Therefore, you'll have to do it for them.

This may actually be the best job-search method of all, so plan carefully. Because your contacts have viewed you competently in the past, chances are better for getting a salary close to what you last earned. And your credentials are already established.

Once you get an interview, don't blow it by whining about your former employer. Don't saddle the dialogue with details of your dismissal or decision to leave the company. Doing so will give too much away. By contrast, you want your business contact to be intrigued with you, and you want his or her impression of you to be one of competence and professionalism. Be oblique about what happened, be good-natured, be upbeat, then get on to how your skills could be of use to him.

One of my clients sent four profile letters off to former business associates, and they resulted in three interviews in the next two weeks. Even though no opening existed at the time, all three were interested in talking to her, and one company actually created a position just for her!

Make a list of the positive professional relationships you've enjoyed during the past three years. The form on the following page provides a method of evaluating them.

Profile contacts

Scan your appointment book and telephone directory for people outside your previous company with whom you did business or worked with (people you genuinely liked and respected). Examine their organizations and industries to see how you might contribute.

Write their names and phone numbers in the first column. Then assess your contacts' influence and power within the respective organizations: Are they in a position to hire you? Would a referral from them mean anything? In the second column, jot down a few words summing up their potential: "CEO," "hot company," "knows everybody," etc. In the third column, rank the potential payoff of that relationship according to the A, B and C priority system. (And remember, contact the A's immediately!)

Contact/ Phone Number	Influence and Power	Rank

Temporary agencies

A tactic often overlooked by job-seekers is to work as a "temp." In the past, temporary agencies only provided clerical and administrative personnel, but today the temp market includes accounting, nursing, dental assistance/hygiene, data processing, etc. All temporary agencies will gladly allow you to move up—from temporary to permanent status—provided that your new employer is willing to pay the accompanying service fee.

Working as a temp allows you to reenter the job market quickly and gives you an opportunity to evaluate the best environment for you. You'll be able to decide firsthand which organizations are best for you. It's like a no-strings-attached audition; if the employer likes you and you like the employer, you may have a match.

Many large temporary agencies actively recruit older adults. They will listen to your concerns and worksite preferences and will do everything they can to make sure temping works for you. Generally, if you're happy, their client will be happy. And then everyone wins.

Substituting

Several people I know secured full-time teaching positions as a result of their exposure as substitute teachers. Again, it's the audition route. The principal, the students and the other teachers all take part in evaluating a new sub's performance. If you do well, you'll have an excellent chance of being hired when a full-time position becomes available.

There are many other businesses and professions that could also use substitute help—that often just make do when someone calls in sick or goes on vacation. But if you are willing to price your services below those charged by temporary agencies, you can build your own substitute or fill-in business.

Be creative: Potential clients for fill-in help include restaurants, hotels, hospitals, retail stores, etc. Most positions are not advertised, so you'll have to do some telephone and drop-in work to identify which jobs could use your skills temporarily. If you show flexibility and keep calling back, you may be called if a need arises. One woman created her own business by providing a fill-in service for dental offices. She had been a dental assistant and front-office person until her boss retired. When she looked for full-time positions, she discovered most dentists wanted someone younger. They wouldn't admit that, of course, but after 12 interviews she got the picture.

She tried a different angle. She remembered how difficult it was in her office whenever someone went on vacation, so she decided to offer that service to dentists in her area. She succeeded. And her business isn't limited to summers: She can work almost year-round if she wishes. Her original plan was to try the temporary route until something permanent was offered. Well, she got her wish and was offered numerous full-time positions. The surprise was that she found she preferred working on a fill-in basis. She avoids the inevitable office politics and can schedule extended time off to visit her grandchildren across the country.

Any of these job-search techniques could be right for you. It depends on which ones you are most comfortable with and which ones you will apply. All have worked for other 50-plus job-seekers. Let us know what works for you!

Chapter Eight

Getting Your *First* Job

What if you're 50 years old and not starting over—but starting out—for the first time? Perhaps you raised your family for 25 years. Perhaps you were in the military. Do the same rules and job-search techniques apply to you? In general, yes. just about everything in this book should apply to you and your job-hunting situation, with just a few important footnotes. That's what this chapter is about.

For starters, you may have no idea what you're getting into. Sure, you may have been privy to your spouse's and friends' job-search war stories, but for the most part you've been sheltered from the impetuousness and complexity of the business world's front lines. Enter this minefield cautiously. It may look harmless, but it's armed and ready. It's there to maximize profits only, and will happily do so at your expense without so much as a nod to casualties.

The homemaker

Let's look at the homemaker first. For years you've probably felt confident and competent on the home front, the PTA front, the soccer front and the social front. But now, as you set out into the workplace, your identity is in question and you may no longer feel so confident.

Your motive for entering the job market could be college for your children or grandchildren, a divorce, a death, the empty-nest syndrome, etc. The first place many homemakers attempt to secure employment is at the local bank, post office, department store or school because they're familiar with these environments.

If you enjoyed a professional career before marriage and children, you may feel this job-search is an adventure, just a lark at first. You may believe the positions you're applying for are beneath your educational experience (but that's OK, you say; you're not looking for a *real* job anyway). Then you're passed over for a simple retail-clerk position, and suddenly a tiny alarm goes off in your head. Next you're rejected for a library-aide's job, and then a UPS delivery position. Bewildered now, fears rise within you. You start thinking about failure, about competition, about rejection.

Because you were productive at home you may assume you will be viewed as a whiz in the work setting—especially for "just a little job." In time, you will be taken seriously—but not yet. So be careful not to move too quickly into job search without thoughtful planning or preparation. Actually, you should be thankful if you don't get any of those first jobs. In essence, you'll have saved yourself from the fate of a dead-end, low-paying abyss.

Let's rewind the tape for a moment. Let's say you do land a job—your first one in 20 years. Ninety percent of the time it will be an entry-level position, perhaps paying 50 cents an hour above minimum wage. After your initial pleasure at having "gotten a job," you may feel resentful at your low wages and the apparent lack of opportunity to advance. And with good reason: Your teenage son probably will be making more per hour than you! Instead of gaining confidence in the world of work, you've just experienced the opposite.

We have counseled dozens of women in this situation—all suburban housewives, all with advanced degrees, all working in low-paying jobs. Do they eventually transfer out of these entry-level quagmires? Some do. Far too many don't. Why don't their employers promote them? Don't they recognize their quality and competence? Absolutely, but not in the way you'd hope. Most employers are so grateful to have a capable person for once in a front-line position who interacts well with clients or customers, they don't want to promote them at all!

There must be a smarter way to enter the work force for the first time—or after a two-decade gap. There is. It's our contention that women who are unaccustomed to working outside the home need an "incubation" period before they go out job-hunting. Let's take a closer look at this idea.

As a homemaker you probably experienced a great deal of freedom and power. You probably made the buying decisions, raised the children, and planned the events and parties. The trade-off is you defined yourself wholly in terms of your husband and children.

An incubation period, therefore, is desirable for several reasons. The most important is that you simply need time and encouragement to redefine yourself and your roles. This isn't an instantaneous process. You will need to learn how to plan rather than react, to compete rather than dictate, to communicate rather than boss. Not an easy assignment. And if you've pictured yourself as the ultimate June Cleaver, you'll also have to learn to let go of your Superwoman attitude. In other words, you need time to develop a new self-image. All of these extremely important issues should be worked out prior to launching any job-search campaign.

During the incubation period, you should work to clarify your goals and values, establish your priorities, and explore career and educational opportunities. You can also use this buffer period to work on your personal appearance: to lose weight, try out new hairstyles, invest in a business wardrobe, etc.

In my opinion, the best incubation device for women is returning to school—whether it's a short-term training program, a two-year certificate course, or a degree. This transition period affords you the most promising opportunity to move successfully from homemaker to employee or businesswoman that I know of. Attending classes and doing assignments will accustom you to schedules and a disciplined regimen.

By contrast, if you go full-steam ahead without setting goals, exploring real career options and training opportunities, you will probably short-change yourself. Not only that, but you may lock yourself into a low-paying track for a good part of your career. Much better to spend a few months or a couple of years organizing yourself first. Then go after what you want—which, by then, you'll know.

Another reason for an incubation period is to prepare and condition your family to get along without you. Your family will have to make some real adjustments. Your husband may even have to learn how to cook. Expect some resentment and some flak. Be compassionate; their worlds are changing as well. You may also experience some guilt, but eventually you'll understand that no alternative is 100 percent perfect or positive. There are trade-offs to staying home and trade-offs to working. But there are also some surprising rewards. Soon you will start to see yourself in a different light—and so will your husband and children.

Steve, a former client of mine, shared this story about his parents with me. Both parents were of Italian descent and the children were raised with traditional family values—his mother stayed home to raise him and his two brothers. Steve's dad, a strong Type-A personality, managed a grocery store. He was sort of a benevolent dictator: What he said, went. Steve's mother was there when the kids came home from school and was supportive and involved in all their activities. Life was predictable.

Then everything changed. At age 50 Steve's father suffered a heart attack, which the doctors attributed to stress. He was off work for six months and was told to reduce his workload and responsibilities when he did return. Since this meant a major loss of income for the family, Steve's mom went into immediate action. She remembered a local bank had been recruiting tellers, so she applied for the job. Although she'd married at 19 and had never worked outside the home, she was hired immediately.

The new arrangement sent a shock wave through the family. Mom had always been home, and Dad had always been the breadwinner. Now their roles reversed. Steve's world became topsy-turvy, too. The crisis changed both parents. Steve's father stopped drinking, smoking and overeating, and he began taking classes in stress management. Soon he began paying more attention to his teenage children. Steve's mother shed 30 pounds, returned to school at night, and earned a bachelor's degree. In five years she was promoted to vice president.

Did the role changes take their toll on the marriage of Steve's parents? Yes, but both parties have accepted those changes. A side benefit is that Steve, now in his mid-20s, had the opportunity to see both his mother and father grow in ways he had never anticipated.

Unfortunately, this story is the exception. More typical is the story of Clare. She married in her early 20s and stayed home to raise her four children. When her husband lost his business at age 50, she was forced to go to work. She returned to the only employer she had ever had—a commercial bakery—and worked there for the next 12 years, enduring poor wages, Saturday work, and physical hardship. Eventually she could no longer do the work and quit. A friend got Clare an interview with her employer, a medium-sized insurance agency, and Clare was hired to do light clerical work.

Today Clare is 66, her children have children of their own, and she can afford to retire. But she won't because she's happier than she's ever been. Clare's story probably qualifies as a happy one, but we just wish the middle of her career could have been happy as well. If she'd only been given the opportunity to incubate for a few months, Clare might have found her career niche 15 years earlier.

One last story. This is about a friend of the family who made the successful transition from homemaker to professional. Sue was married to a man 15 years her senior. He died of cancer at the age of 62, and Sue was left with four daughters to raise. Thankfully, money was not a pressing issue, so she chose to stay home for the next six years until her youngest was in high school. At age 48 she entered a master's program in adult career-counseling. She interned at a private college and was hired as a counselor after graduation. Today, she earns good money and finds her work satisfying and challenging. Her incubation period (a two-year educational program) gave her a chance to regroup, plan the rest of her life and become empowered.

If you can't afford the time or money to return to school full-time, you should, at the very least, participate in a career-planning workshop. They are available through community colleges, adult-education programs, parks-and-recreation departments, and learning exchanges. Most are free. If you need a job quickly, here are some other options you may want to consider:

Sales. Boundless opportunities exist for mature men and women in sales. But you'll need to know something about sales before you embark, of course. Look in the yellow pages for learning exchanges and continuing-education classes and enroll in a short-term sales-training program (often only 10 to 25 hours). If you have more time, community colleges offer semester-long sales courses as well. (You'd be surprised at how many middle-aged and older people enroll in these classes.) Read books or listen to tapes on sales and pay attention to how salespeople sell to you. What do you like and dislike about their techniques? What would you do differently?

There are hundreds of base (guaranteed amount of dollars per month) plus commission positions available right in your community—everything from drapery sales to business machines to office products to furniture. If people have always told you "You should be in sales," why not consider it? And the beauty of sales is, there's no discrimination. No one cares about your sex, color or age. If you produce, you're coveted. Period. Amen.

Five years ago, we purchased a lovely home. We were driving down a street one day and just fell in love with it. Not having an agent, we called the real-estate agent listed on the "For Sale" sign, and she turned out to be a friendly woman named Evelyn. She agreed to show us the house, and we set up a time to meet. At the designated time Evelyn appeared with her husband, Harry, and her secretary. Harry had retired years before, but Evelyn often took him with her on sales calls to keep her company. Evelyn was at least 70 years old.

She became our agent and represented both sides in the transaction. She was honest and thorough, returned phone calls immediately, and when escrow closed, brought us some lovely German wine glasses and a case of wine. A few months later we were invited to her home for a party. In her den were four walls covered with sales awards and plaques. Only then did we learn she had entered real estate in her mid-60s!

Last year, when friends of ours were grumbling about their real-estate agent, we told them about Evelyn. They were as pleased with her as we had been. (Women, by the way, tend to do well in sales because they've been trained to nurture and listen—skills that pay off handsomely in sales.)

Childcare. This is another option that requires little training or formal education. Childcare centers are in desperate need of quality day-care workers. The vast majority would love to hire caring women in their 50s and 60s. Typically, the pay is only slightly above minimum wage, but if you take classes in childhood development, the pay can jump to $8 or $10 an hour. All studies point to day-care as being a strong employment field throughout the 1990s.

Own service business. Two service businesses in particular are becoming more prevalent these days as working adults have less and less discretionary time: errand/shopping services, and sick-child baby-sitting services. The first requires no inventory and simple advertising. Most families could use assistance with shopping, getting Billy to the dentist, taking the dog to the vet, staying home for the repair man, etc.

Two 50-plus women we know offer a shopping service—not for groceries but for special gifts. Clients give them information about who the gift is for and a price range—and the rest is up to them! They also wrap and deliver the gift.

The second is a sick-child baby-sitting service. You stay home with someone's child so the mother can go to work.

Once you think about it, there are many possibilities. Jot down some others in the space below.

1. _____
2. _____
3. _____
4. _____
5. _____

The veteran

Now let's look at the military person-turned-civilian. The armed forces is a special world with its own parameters of conduct, dress, rank, discipline, etc. Many of your needs and wants (food, clothing, housing, security) were taken care of. No longer. Therefore, you may be in for a real culture shock as you maneuver into the contemporary job market. If the business world seems unfriendly, it's because it doesn't know what to make of you—or what to do with you.

Just as the reentering homemaker could benefit from an incubation period, so should you consider a debriefing period before you jump into the civilian job-search arena. You, too, will be more effective in your career search if you take a needed breather. The best preparation for life on the outside is to take courses off-base and participate in civilian activities as much as possible.

Unless you've attained a high rank, though, don't count on anyone getting too excited by your military background. Probably just the opposite. In the civilian world you'll have to overcome a double-whammy of stereotypes: the older person and the military person. In the business world the perception of the military is a mixed bag: On the plus side is patriotism, on the minus side is the perception that because you're used to a heavy dose of structure, rules and regulations, you won't be effective in a less-structured or nonstructured environment.

During your debriefing period define what you want to do, what you can do, what organizations would be interested in your abilities, and which ones are more structured than others. I also recommend enrollment in a training or educational program to update your skills and broaden your interests. This will give you the opportunity to interact in a group setting, on a give-and-take basis, where rank means nothing.

Every occupation and industry has its own jargon, and the military has more than its share. To succeed in civilian life, you'll also need to eliminate the *militar-ese* from your speech.

It has been my experience that private nonprofits (Red Cross, Boy Scouts, chambers of commerce, etc.) are more accepting of career military persons than mainstream businesses. So you might try these first. Also, think of ways to transfer what you learned in the military to civilian life. One retired Air Force pilot I know does helicopter traffic reports for an all-news radio station—a position he has held for the last 12 years.

Whatever path you choose, if you work to make your transition a smooth one, you will join the hundreds of thousands of homemakers and veterans who have successfully entered—or returned to—the business world.

Part Three

Polish and Preparation

Chapter Nine

Enhancing Your Image

Many times, job-seekers call excitedly, saying they have been called by Such-and-Such Company for an interview. But before congratulations are offered they move on to, "I can't possibly be qualified for that job. There's no way they'll ever hire me."

Think about it. If an employer has 100 applications for each job opening, has read through all of them, has narrowed his or her selections down to 10, and you are one of the 10, then *you are qualified*. It is not your job to second-guess the employer on your qualifications.

Don't spend the bulk of the interview, therefore, trying to convince the employer that you have the right skills and experience for the job. He or she already knows that. Your assignment during the interview is twofold: 1) Project a professional upbeat image, and 2) talk benefits—what about *you* will make life easier, more productive, more exciting and more profitable for him or her. (More about "benefit selling" in the next chapter.)

Let's talk about image first. It's a concept everyone (small business, government, large corporation) is concerned with.

121

Admittedly it's a buzz word, but it represents a valid concern for the employer. You need to understand, therefore, what image is all about and how to project yourself in the best possible light.

If you think about the things that contribute to one's image, you may decide, as we have, that there are four distinct ingredients: *appearance, values, competence* and *behavior*. The job of the personnel department or assigned interviewer is, bottom line, to decide if the image you project is the one the organization wants to buy.

Appearance

Appearance is probably the easiest of the image ingredients to control. You will want to project an upbeat professional appearance, so invest in a new outfit, including shoes. (If you are applying for a government job, do not overdress. It will intimidate those who are interviewing you.) If you are a woman, make sure you project competence, not cuteness. Frills and ruffles, head-to-toe pastels and/or exaggerated color-coordination translate into "cute." If you're applying for an administrative or secretarial position, you might get away with cute attire, but not if you're interviewing for a managerial or executive position.

If you are a man applying for a professional position, dress in a suit or coat and tie. It doesn't matter if you were allowed or encouraged to wear baggy pants and Hush Puppies in your last job: This is a new ball game. Further, don't make the mistake of dressing like the people already working for the firm. They work there; you are being interviewed. It's a significant difference.

Whether you are male or female, follow these rules when assembling an interview outfit: 1) Dress for where you want to be, not for where you are now; 2) Spend more money for your clothes than you normally would—the investment will pay off handsomely later; 3) Dress conservatively, but not in a matronly or old-fashioned style; and 4) Wear natural fibers: wool, cotton, silk. Stay away from 100 percent polyester clothing; it doesn't breathe and after several wearings it loses its crispness.

Incorporate a bounce or a flair into your interview outfit. By this I mean a subtle sign that you're different and interesting. In all likelihood, if they're interested, you will be asked back for a second and, perhaps, a third interview. Therefore, you will need to assemble two or three quality outfits. The basic question you should ask yourself is, "Do I look as upbeat and professional as I possibly can?"

Next, think about how you want to look. Scan magazines for pictures of models who project the image you want for yourself. Study their clothing and grooming. Cut the pictures out and put them on your refrigerator or somewhere to remind yourself of the image you want to project in your job search.

Appearance also means grooming, hairstyle, makeup and how you put yourself together. Think of yourself as a wonderful gift you're presenting to a potential employer. No matter how outstanding you are, you will appear even better if you're wrapped in a lovely package. Women, don't date yourself with a hairstyle you wore back in 1970. The same holds true for makeup: the heavy powdered look is long gone, so are penciled-in eyebrows. Styles change. Project a contemporary image, an image of someone who welcomes, rather than resists, change. Men, you may not want to look like you've just stepped out of *GQ* but you must look crisp, well-groomed and contemporary in your dress.

Many department stores have personal shoppers who will help you assemble an appropriate work wardrobe. Their services are generally free. Tell the personal shopper what your budget is, what position(s) you are applying for, and allow him or her to pull several different outfits together for you. It can save you money in the long run, and you'll be confident knowing you will look your best.

What does your appearance say about you? What, if anything, would you like to change about the way you look? Write your thoughts below.

Pluses (what I like about my appearance):

Clothes: _____

Hairstyle: _____

Makeup/Grooming: _____

Overall: _____

Minuses (things I must improve or change):

Clothes: _____

Hairstyle: _____

Makeup/Grooming: _____

Overall: _____

Values

Values constitute the second image ingredient. They are what we stand for—our belief system (self-reliance, personal integrity, status, family first, spiritual growth, achievements, independence, security, whatever). Values motivate us and guide us. The employer must decide if you will enhance or hurt the organization. Are you an employee who will disappear at exactly 5:00 p.m., or will you be there to answer the phone at 5:08 p.m.? Will you give more than a full day's work for a full day's pay?

The employer will try to assess your values by asking "self-knowledge" questions: "What is your greatest strength? Your greatest weakness?"

What are your values? Are they reflected in your behavior? Which of them do you want to convey to the interviewer? How will you do that?

Value	**How I plan to convey it**
1. _____	_____
2. _____	_____
3. _____	_____
4. _____	_____
5. _____	_____

Competence

Competence is the third image ingredient the employer will assess. Your competence means your skills, so you may be asked technical questions about your area(s) of expertise. The employer is simply trying to gauge your skill level. Your responses should be crisp and well-organized. Don't repeat yourself or talk the subject into the ground. Again, your qualifications are already a given. Now, it's just a matter of presenting that knowledge in a persuasive manner.

Take a moment to evaluate your skills. Some are generic (most employers will be interested in them), but some will interest only specific employers. Which ones are these? They are the ones you want to accentuate. List them next.

Employer 1: _____

Skill 1. _____
Skill 2. _____
Skill 3. _____

Employer 2: _____

Skill 1. _____
Skill 2. _____
Skill 3. _____

Employer 3: _____

Skill 1. _____
Skill 2. _____
Skill 3. _____

Employer 4: _____

Skill 1. _____
Skill 2. _____
Skill 3. _____

Employer 5: _____

Skill 1. _____
Skill 2. _____
Skill 3. _____

How did your colleagues generally judge your skills when you worked? How did your supervisors? List these as well.

Colleagues' evaluation: _____

_____

Bosses' evaluation: _____

_____

Behavior

The final image ingredient is behavior. How you come across in terms of likability, a positive attitude and willingness to share information is how your behavior will be assessed. As businesses continue to downsize, hiring a new employee takes on new seriousness. It is not uncommon to be asked to meet with four to eight different players before a job offer is tendered. More than ever before, businesses are making sure that the person they hire will be a welcome asset to the team—hence everyone's input.

So stride into the interview room confidently, shoulders straight, head high. Smile, offer your hand to the interviewer, and introduce yourself clearly and calmly. Believe it or not, at this moment, much of the final outcome has already been settled.

The quickest way to kill an interview is to patronize the interviewer. So, none of those "When I was your age" routines. The interviewer, regardless of age, has already achieved some status in the organization. Quite obviously, it is not your place to tell him or her that your experience is somehow superior. Several years ago, Terry conducted a two-week training session in Northern California for reentry workers. One gentleman insisted on addressing him as "youngster," as in "Good morning, youngster." By the third day, he was grinding his teeth and finally told him, privately, that although he was younger than the gentleman, he was no youngster. The older man had no idea he'd been offensive or patronizing in any way. So think out your responses in advance and be sensitive to how your answers will sound to someone younger than yourself.

Does your behavior indicate that you're a professional? Are you upbeat and positive? How do you think others perceive your behavior? (You'll need to decipher the feedback.) Is there anything about your behavior you would like to change?

Your perception of your behavior: _____

_____

Others' perception of your behavior: _____

_____

What you would change about your behavior: _____

_____

The interviewer is trying to accomplish two tasks—both of which have to do with image. First, he or she is trying to assess your image. Do your appearance, values, competence and behavior work together to make a coherent whole, or is one ingredient somehow fighting another? In other words, is there a glitch in the system called *you*? Do you verbally have no problem proclaiming yourself a professional, yet dress or act unprofessionally?

Second, the interviewer is trying to determine if your image will enhance the organization. The interviewer's reputation is on the line: His or her selection is a direct reflection on him or her. If the choice is a winner, his or her status in the company will rise; a loser (especially if this is a repeat performance) will diminish his or her reputation. Because the interviewer must be cautious, you must do everything you can to persuade him or her that you are someone who will not only do the job but will make that interviewer look good as a result.

Chapter Ten

Selling Your Benefits

In the previous chapter, you learned that your success at job search depends on how well you present a professional and appealing image; i.e., how well you wrapped, displayed or packaged *you* (the product). In this chapter we'll discuss how you can sell yourself. If what you offer draws enough interest to get an interview, you will have moved your customer (the employer) from the browsing stage to the buying stage. Your job then will be to close the sale, to make sure he or she buys your talents. Give the employer a good reason to buy, and you'll get a job offer. The trick is finding which benefits motivate which employer.

Salespeople quickly learn that what sells steak is the sizzle and what sells $15 tubes of lipstick is the dream of glamour and romance. Although as buyers we try to justify our purchases with rational explanations, the truth is, we usually don't buy a car because of its gas mileage or its engine size. The real reason we buy a Volkswagen or Lexus is how we perceive ourselves and how we think a particular car fits in with or enhances our lifestyle. We buy a car for what it will do for us, not what it's made out of—or even if it has passenger-side air bags.

The hiring decision is an emotional buying decision, too; in fact, much more emotional than most will admit. The employer will hire you if you appeal to his view of himself (open-minded, nonconventional, tough, whatever). How will you know how the employer views himself? (Reread Chapter 5 on personality types.) Then pay close attention to the visual and verbal clues the employer displays in the interview and respond accordingly.

Appealing to an interviewer's buying motives means turning your particular traits and experiences into buying/hiring reasons for that employer. Salespeople are trained to conduct a features-advantages-benefits analysis of their product before they ever try to sell it. In this situation, you are your product and it's time you analyzed your features, advantages and benefits.

Features are the facts. In and of themselves they are neither good nor bad; they just are. A product's features include color, materials, warranty, cost, etc. Still, not all features are of interest to all buyers. Have you ever walked into an electronics store and had an aggressive salesperson bombard you with 101 features about a new CD system—when all you wanted was to listen to its sound? The same holds true in interviewing: If you just present a lengthy list of experiences and skills without first finding out what the employer really needs or wants, you won't get his or her attention. No attention, no second interview...and no job offer.

Turning features into benefits involves three important steps. First, you must choose which features to stress. Actually, you may have to refine your feature selection several times: 1) When you analyze the job description and respond with a cover letter; 2) when you prepare for the interview; and, 3) during the interview itself when some features draw a positive response and others don't. But you can only be flexible and responsive in an interview if you are fully prepared. So, while features-advantages-benefits preparation may seem like a lot of work, it is well worth it. Remember, there are no retakes in the interview business. Your one shot in front of the interviewer must be your best shot.

The second step in selling your benefits is to translate your features into advantages. An advantage is really an explanation of the feature: what the feature means and/or does. Although advantages are a little more intriguing than features, they still won't get you a job offer.

The third and most important step is translating your advantages into benefits the employer cares about. Here's an example: Let's say you are a reentry woman. You have been home for the past 25 years raising your children and have gone through a divorce recently. What can you offer an employer who wants a take-charge office manager? Start with the fact that you are divorced and your children are grown. With a little creativity, this could be a significant benefit to almost any employer: "I am divorced and my children are grown (feature). I am at a place in my life where I can and want to put all my energy into a career (advantage). If you hire me, you will get a totally dedicated and motivated employee who knows how to run things—I ran a household for 25 years and did it very well. I will apply those same skills to running your office, and I guarantee I'll not only make your business more profitable, but I'll also make your life a whole lot easier" (benefit). Now you've succeeded in getting the employer's attention!

Had you only said you were divorced with grown children, you would have left the important translation up to the employer. Then it would be a coin-flip as to whether that person would have been able to construe your single status as a strength or a weakness. Why leave it to chance?

True, some interviewers are on your side and will visualize you in the position you're applying for with all your articulated and unarticulated strengths. But many employers can't—unless you literally draw a picture for them. Again, you have to supply the sizzle.

Let's try another situation: You are a retired engineer who wants to go back to work. The obvious selling point is: "I've been an engineer for 20 years (feature). My judgments are based on experience as well as books (advantage). Because I understand engineering backward and forward, you won't have to spend a lot of time or money training me. I can be up and running on a project immediately" (benefit).

As you assemble your resume package and prepare for the interview, think, eat and sleep benefits. If you do, you'll stand a good chance of capturing the employer's interest. Take the time before every interview to do a complete features-advantages-benefits analysis. Think about what the business does and what benefits in your application, resume or cover letter piqued the firm's initial interest (more on how to prepare these in the next chapter). Play those up in the interview while monitoring the employer's interest and response level.

Also helpful: During the interview imagine a bright neon sign that flashes "So what?" is implanted in the interviewer's forehead. This obnoxious sign will continue to flash if you go into a litany of features. So when the employer asks you, "Why should I hire you?" think of the neon sign and talk benefits!

It would be nice if all the features about ourselves were positive. But chances are they aren't. Don't be afraid to deal with neutral or negative features. The interviewer will be thinking about them anyway, so you might as well try to convert them as well as you can to advantages and benefits. For example, let's say you've been unemployed for two years. The employer knows it and you know it.

Rather than act defensively, take the offensive: "I've been unemployed for the past two years (feature), and to be honest, at first I thought my world had fallen apart. But the last two years have been good to me. They've given me a perspective and an opportunity to do some soul-searching (advantage). And you know what? I discovered I really didn't want to go back to what I'd been doing for 20 years. So I took some career-exploration courses and found out my skills, interests and talents lay in drafting instead. Now I'm fully trained and ready to embark on a new career. I've never been more enthused in my life! If you hire me, you'll be hiring someone who loves what he does, and it will show" (benefit).

Got the idea? Now it's your turn. On the following page is a features-advantages-benefits worksheet. Make extra copies so you can make up a fresh analysis for every job you pursue. This will keep you focused on what you can do for the employer instead of what the employer can do for you. As corny as it sounds, the employer is tuned to only one radio station: W.I.I.F.M. ("What's In It For Me?"). Answer that question, and you'll get the job offer!

Features-Advantages-Benefits worksheet

Directions: Features are facts about you (your experience, your skills, your training, your education, etc.). Convert them into advantages and benefits that will be significant to the employer.

Feature (fact)	**Advantage** (what it means)	**Benefit** (what's in it for the employer)

Chapter Eleven

Profiling Your Merits

The point of the application, resume and cover letter is to get you an interview. That is a very tall order. So if you've allocated 30 hours to job search every week, you'll need to spend 10 to 15 hours unearthing job leads and the remaining 15 to 20 hours developing resume packages for specific employers.

No one likes to spend time on resumes and cover letters, and that can work to your advantage. In fact, an amazing percentage of job applicants so dislike this task that they invest the bare minimum in terms of time and effort, sending in resumes and cover letters that are unfocused and filled with sloppy syntax. The best way to differentiate yourself from everyone else, therefore, is to make your resume package persuasive and competent. This chapter will teach you how to accomplish both tasks.

Let's start by defining some terms. The "resume package" can include a job application, a resume and a cover letter, but it really depends on how the employer defines the term. In almost all cases employers will request a resume. An application may or may not be part of the required package.

As a rule of thumb, public-sector employers more often require a completed application than do private-sector businesses. But check anyway. Help-wanted ads may ask for a "letter of application," a "letter of interest" or a "cover letter." They are all names for the same thing: a letter introducing you and spelling out what you have to offer.

If you are applying for a mid-level or higher position, you probably will be asked to complete an application only after a first interview or, in some cases, after you have been offered the position. Since every employer handles applications differently, prepare a master and take it with you at all times on your job search. It will serve as a guide to help you fill out an application on the spot, reducing the chances of omitted or forgotten information, inconsistent or incorrect data, or messiness (i.e., since you're just copying information, not writing off the top of your head, you'll cut down on erasures and cross-outs).

This is an important detail to remember because the application is often used as a screening device, and if it's completed haphazardly or sloppily, the potential employer may immediately form negative thoughts about your abilities.

On the other hand, if the application and cover letter are well done and persuasive, and if the resume is tailored to the job description and exhibits the required experience and skills, you should be asked in for an interview. While employers will never admit they are judging you substantially on the way your package is wrapped, they are. After all, they really have nothing else on which to base their impressions. We cannot stress too strongly how unscientific and emotion-laden the process of personnel selection really is. But until the process undergoes a dramatic overhaul, it's all we've got.

The application

Although the application is a legally binding document, that does not mean you should provide the personnel department with reasons *not* to interview or hire you. In the last 10 to 15 years, the Supreme Court has strongly ruled in favor of employee rights. In practice this means most employers are cautious about what they say about former employees. Most large organizations will only verify time of employment and ending salary. If you have a skeleton or two in your career closet, therefore, don't be too concerned; chances are a potential employer will never learn about it.

Don't leave anything blank on the application. Treat it as if it were a written test: Read it over carefully before filling it out, and follow all directions. If a space or line doesn't apply to your situation, write "N/A." Usually, you will be asked to print your responses. If you're allowed to, take the application with you rather than completing it there. We all make mistakes, so it is smart to go to the nearest copy machine and make one or two copies of it. Then spend some time completing a copy as carefully as possible.

Only when you are sure you have filled in each space correctly, completely and beneficially, should you transcribe the information on to the original application. This is more work, of course, but now your application will work for, rather than against, you. In addition, it will provide you with a reason to return to personnel. The more times they see you, the greater the chance they'll get to know, and like, you.

There are usually some questions on the application that may be tough or tricky to answer. On the following pages we've provided a few ideas on how to complete the most ambiguous.

At the end of the chapter is a standard application for you to complete. But *wait!* Before you touch it, make a copy. Think your answers out carefully before you write them. Have someone you respect read it for clarity and make any needed changes. Then fill out your master application.

Position: Already the ambiguities begin. Even if you are not applying for a specific job opening, be as specific as you can here. Our rationale is that if the personnel department finds your application desirable, it will want to forward it to the appropriate department. So you'll have to, at the very least, indicate a department or function. If there *is* a specific opening, clearly identify it here.

Date you can start: Tell the truth. Since you presumably are not working, chances are you would like to start as soon as possible. Therefore: "ASAP," "Immediately" or "Flexible" are all appropriate answers. Don't worry about the employer perceiving you as too anxious. If you are seriously seeking employment, let it show.

Salary desired: Downplay the money issue. Write either "Negotiable" or "Open." If you are changing occupations, you may have to begin your new career at a lower salary. Of course, your new career might pay more than your last position. In either scenario, it's best not to label yourself in terms of money.

May we inquire of your present employer: If you are not working, write "N/A." If you are working, write "Only if job offer is pending." That way, you protect your present position until the last possible moment—and until you have received a conditional offer from the new employer.

Date graduated: Because employers are not allowed to practice age discrimination, the application will not out-and-out ask your age. But it can easily be calculated when you fill out this line under the "Education" portion. You have two choices here: You can write "N/A" or you can insert the actual date, telling yourself if this organization discriminates, you don't want to work for it anyway. I strongly suggest you do the former because, once again, the sole purpose of the application is to get you an interview.

Hobbies, clubs and activities: Think about the type of position you are applying for and figure out which hobbies, clubs and activities would enhance your credibility. For example, salespeople need to be people-oriented. Therefore, if you are applying for a sales position, list organizations you belong to (or will soon join) and indicate you have a competitive nature and enjoy the good things in life: "Am active in three sales leads clubs, Rotary, and the Chamber of Commerce. Belong to Fair Oaks Country Club and play golf there every Saturday."

On the other hand, if you are applying for a teaching position, indicate you are well-read, enjoy research and all aspects of teaching: "Am a Hemingway buff and active member of Friends of Hemingway Foundation. Tutor in a community literacy program and am writing a book on local folklore for Springtown's Historical Society." Although you can stretch the truth a little here, don't go overboard. If your interviewer turns out to be a real Hemingway aficionado, you'd better be able to back up what you wrote.

Why would you like this job: Think back on features-advantages-benefits and write out a statement that translates your qualifications, experience and skills into a benefit for the employer. Your aim here is to convey a win-win scenario: The employer wins because you can solve his or her need; you win because you want to work for the very best in the industry.

Salaries in former positions: Go with the highest monthly salary you ever grossed in that position. If you wish, add the value of the benefit package to your monthly salary. If you suspect the position you're applying for offers considerably less money than what you were making, however, you may wish to write "N/A" instead.

Reason for leaving: Always word this in a positive manner. Never use negative statements like: "Was fired" or "Disagreement with boss." Instead, use "Returned home to care for family," "Corporate merger," "Career change," "Returned to school" or "Left for a higher-paying position."

References: Use the strongest references you have, preferably professional people. Make sure you check with them *before* you use them as references, though. Use colleagues and associates when appropriate. If you know someone well within the company you are applying to, use that person's name—but first check out his or her reputation there! Use solid local people as a first choice, because personnel people are less likely to make long-distance calls to check on references.

Physical record: If you have a health or physical impairment that would hinder your ability to do the job, you really should mention it here. But if you have a handicap or a condition that is not relevant to this job, don't. Use the most upbeat phraseology possible: "Am in great physical health!"

The resume

Consider the resume a personal advertisement of your qualifications to prospective employers. As such, you should (and are expected to) put your best foot forward, generalize and combine experience, and even stretch the truth—just a little bit. Once again, the purpose of the resume is to get you an interview. Like a good ad, the resume should be concise, no more than two pages. It should be visually appealing, and it should intrigue the employer enough that you'll be invited in for a closer look.

There are several categories of information you will want to address in your resume. They include: Career Objective, Work Experience, Education, Affiliations/Committees, Training, Special Abilities/Skills, and References. At the end of the chapter, you'll find a suggested format, followed by a filled-in example. The format helps you see things from the employer's perspective. Basically, you are attempting to answer the employer's primary question: "Why are you qualified for this position?" Therefore, every word you write should be a clear response to that unspoken question.

Literally hundreds of books have been written about resumes alone. You can spend weeks studying the pros and cons of each format and still not be any closer to getting an interview—much less a job offer. The resume format in this book works. Hundreds of our clients have used it who have not only gotten interviews, they have gotten jobs. Because the employer is inundated with every kind of resume from the pretentious to the sloppy—yours will stand out with its clean lines and simple, clear prose.

Now let's go through the resume, line by line. Start at the top with a clearly stated *Career Objective:* "Sales Representative," "Store Manager," "Computer Technician," etc.

Don't be vague here; don't write something like "An opportunity to utilize my marketing skills in a growth-oriented manufacturing firm."

Next is *Work Experience.* If yours is sketchy or you've changed jobs frequently, downplay this section by combining some of your work experience and/or omitting dates from employment summaries. A reverse chronological (most recent job first) resume works best if your employment history is an asset. Format your work experience by listing your title or position first, followed by responsibilities, and below that, achievements. Follow these with the name and location (city and state only, not street address) of the business and, if beneficial to you, dates of employment or years employed.

Make sentences short and punchy; don't weigh each concept down with details. On the other hand, try to use specific numbers when appropriate. They add credibility to your claims. Use action words, and avoid the pronoun "I" when listing your responsibilities and achievements. For example:

141

Sales Representative. Aggressively sold hardware and software test programs to 80+ school districts from Bakersfield to Oregon border. Exceeded sales quota every quarter and was chosen Salesperson of the Year for three consecutive years, 1988-90.

XYZ Corporation
San Francisco, CA
1990-1993

Employers look for dependability, likability and competence. So make sure you convey these characteristics when describing your responsibilities and achievements. An example of *dependability* would be "Opened and closed the store every working day for five years." *Likability* can be summed up by "Selected as group leader for a 35-person research project," which shows that you were well thought-of, liked by your peers, and that you exhibited leadership qualities. *Competence* could be illustrated by statements like "Chosen to represent company at industry-wide convention" or "Selected to deliver keynote address at industry convention for three consecutive years." The point is, simply stating you are dependable, likable and/or competent doesn't work; providing lively examples of how you possess those characteristics does, and they will catch the employer's attention.

If your work experience is limited, use a one-page resume. If one page would short-change your credentials or experience, use two pages—but no more. Since most candidates try to limit their resumes to one page, using a page-and-a-half to two pages can attract more attention but only if your experience warrants it. Anything beyond two pages is too much for an employer to skim.

Do not put personal information on your resume (it detracts from your professionalism). And don't list references. Instead, under *References* write "Available upon request."

It goes without saying that your resume must be neatly word-processed and error-free. It should be copied or printed on heavy (60-pound) bond paper. If you are mailing it, include a cover letter.

The cover letter

The purpose of the cover letter is to introduce yourself to a prospective employer. While you're at it, you should highlight your past achievements as well as what you can specifically do for *this* company.

If you are targeting several different industries or applying for different occupations, you will most likely need to construct several different resumes. If, however, you are targeting one specific field and believe your new resume represents you well, use the same basic cover letter for all resume requests.

The cover letter gives you an opportunity to stress some relevant features-advantages-benefits to specific employers. For example, you hear about a job that involves public speaking. In your resume you already state you're a member of Toastmasters International and enjoy public speaking—but it's buried among a lot of other activities. For this particular employer, you need it up front and highlighted. Rather than rewriting your resume to punch up this information, highlight it in your cover letter thusly: "In addition to my speechwriting skills, I have been an active member of Toastmasters International for the past six years. I know my public speaking abilities and stand-up presentation skills would enhance XYZ's image in the marketplace."

If the employer is advertising the position through a P.O. Box, send a cover letter with a resume. If the employer asks you to bring the resume to the place of business, include a cover letter anyway. Although cover letters are time-consuming to write, they are well worth it.

Basically, the cover letter should comprise three parts: *Part One* defines why you are writing and how you learned about the position. Keep this brief (one or two sentences). *Part Two* tells why you believe you have the necessary qualifications to do the job well. This is the bulk of the letter—the sales portion. Here you will translate your prior work or volunteer experience, education and training into tangible benefits for the employer. *Part Three* requests an interview and thanks the employer for his/her consideration. Again, make this short and sweet.

Study the example on page 150, then write one of your own using the suggested format.

PERSONAL INFORMATION—(please print)

Date: _____   Social Security
                                  number: _____

Name _____
          Last   First   Middle

Present address _____
              Street   City   State   Zip

Telephone number _____

Referred by_____

_ _

EMPLOYMENT DESIRED
                          Date you   Salary
Position _____ can start _____ desired _____

Are you employed now? _____   If so, may we inquire
                                of your present employer? _____

Ever applied to this
company before? _____   Where _____When _____

_ _

EDUCATION

High school_____
        Name   Location   Date graduated

College _____
        Name   Location   Major/Minor Date graduated

Trade school
etc. _____
        Name   Location   Major/Minor Date graduated

Subjects of special study
or research work _____

What foreign languages
do you speak fluently? _____Read?_____Write?_____

Hobbies, clubs & activities _____

_ _

IN YOUR OWN HANDWRITING, WRITE WHY YOU WOULD LIKE THIS

JOB _____
_____
_____

FORMER EMPLOYERS (List last four employers, starting with last one)

Name and address
of employer _____ Date began _____
Date ended _____ Salary _____
Summarize your duties _____ Reason for leaving _____
_____
_____

Name and address
of employer _____ Date began _____
Date ended _____ Salary _____
Summarize your duties _____ Reason for leaving _____
_____
_____

Name and address
of employer _____ Date began _____
Date ended _____ Salary _____
Summarize your duties _____ Reason for leaving _____
_____
_____

Name and address
of employer _____ Date began _____
Date ended _____ Salary _____
Summarize your duties _____ Reason for leaving _____
_____
_____

REFERENCES (Provide the names, addresses and telephone numbers of three persons not related to you whom you have known for at least one year.)

1. _____
   Name   Address   Telephone
2. _____
   Name   Address   Telephone
3. _____
   Name   Address   Telephone

PHYSICAL RECORD (Describe any impairment that would interfere with your ability to perform the job for which you have applied.)

_____
_____

I authorize investigation of all statements contained in this application. I understand that misrepresentation or omission of facts is cause for dismissal. Further, I understand and agree that my employment is for no definite period and may, regardless of the date of payment of my wages and salary, be terminated at any time without any previous notice.

Date _____ Signature _____

RESUME FORMAT

Name
Street address
City, State, and Zip
Home phone number (H)
Work phone number (W-if applicable)

CAREER OBJECTIVE: (Put a specific job title here)
Qualified by

WORK EXPERIENCE:
Title or position. Responsibilities included:

(List achievements & awards after each bullet)
-
-
-

Name of business, location, dates of employment (or number of years)

Title or position. Responsibilities included:

Name of business, location, dates of employment (or number of years)

(Continue to list work experience for 15-20 years)

EDUCATION/AFFILIATIONS/COMMITTEES: College degree, major, name of college. Leave out organizations that specify **race**, religion or politics *unless* relevant to position sought.

TRAINING: Recent training that is relevant to the position for which you are applying.

SPECIAL SKILLS/ABILITIES:

REFERENCES: Available upon request.

Jill Smith
123 Shady Lane
Anytown, USA 12345
213-555-1234 (H)
213-555-1235 (W)

CAREER OBJECTIVE: Educational Sales Representative

Qualified by

WORK EXPERIENCE:

Sales Representative. Responsibilities included selling educational hardware, software and consulting services to school districts in California from Monterey County to the Oregon border.
- Sold more than any other salesperson in the Western Territory in 1991.
- Received several awards for outstanding sales performance.
- Received national recognition for sales in two of three possible categories.

National Computer Systems, Los Angeles, California, 1990 to present

Partner, Director of Marketing/Sales. TMC specializes in sales training and marketing consulting. In addition, TMC represents several educational products and offers management-development training to business and public agencies. Responsibilities included marketing services and products to private businesses and public agencies.
- Sold public training contracts to agencies of the Federal Government. Contract total over five years in excess of $3 million.
- Marketing Director for a $10.4 million townhome complex for six months to reverse downward sales spiral.
- Marketing Director (consultant, six months) for educational products company. Recruited, trained and managed sales staff to get new company off the ground.

The Marketing Concern, Oakland, CA, 1983 to 1990

High School English Teacher and Department Chairperson.
- Initiated a number of innovative programs that decreased costs and provided unique learning experiences for students.

Director of Federally Funded Training Programs
- Developed, directed and managed a host of programs for youth and adults. Programs included Summer Youth, Adult and Youth Work Experience, and Vocational Classroom Training.

Proficiency High School, Sacramento, CA, 1965 to 1983

ADDITIONAL EXPERIENCE:
Co-hosted, wrote and directed an hour-long television program entitled "Focusing on Drug Abuse."

Developed sales-training programs with the Sacramento Chamber of Commerce and Mill Valley Community College to provide trained youth for local businesses.

EDUCATION/AFFILIATIONS/COMMITTEES:

B.B.A.: Business, emphasis in Accounting, Marketing and Economics; California State University, San Jose
Postgraduate Studies: California State University, Sacramento
Stanford Home for Children—Board of Directors
Sacramento Chamber of Commerce-Economic Development Committee
Roseville Chamber of Commerce—Governmental Action Committee
Project Review Commission—City of Roseville, Chairperson
Oakland Chamber of Commerce—Ambassadors Club
Placer County Mental Health Board
Placer County Technical Advisory Committee on Drug Abuse

REFERENCES:Available upon request.

COVER LETTER

Current Date (about 1 inch from top of paper)

Mr. John Jones
John Jones Associates
111 Main Street
Anytown, USA 12345

Dear Mr. Jones:

Please accept this letter and the accompanying resume as my application for the educational sales representative position recently announced in *The Sanctose Mercury*.

I am uniquely qualified for this position because of my excellent sales background and my thorough knowledge of the educational market. First, I am a recent employee of National Computer Systems, selling educational products to school districts throughout Northern California. As a first-year salesperson, I sold a greater dollar volume than any other salesperson in the Western Region and received several awards for my outstanding production.

Second, I have more than 18 years' continuous employment with a Sacramento area school district. I began my career in public education as a teacher, was promoted to counselor and then to the administration team. I understand the way schools work, budgeting, and the steps in the purchasing process. Probably most important, I understand the pace at which schools move and the necessity for a calm, professional sales presentation.

Finally, I have more than five years' experience selling and teaching selling techniques to other professionals. When I resigned from public-school employment, I began my own marketing consulting and sales-training business. I have since successfully sold services to businesses and public agencies throughout California.

In addition, I have excellent written and oral presentation skills. I make a good first impression and have the knowledge and experience to present to groups of all sizes in a professional manner.

I look forward to talking with you and learning more about this exciting opportunity.

Sincerely,

Jill Smith

Jill Smith

Part Four

The Interview

Chapter Twelve

Bucking Stereotypes

Bluntly put, stereotyping is putting people into boxes so we don't have to deal with them as individuals. If you allow interviewers to put you in the "older worker" box, you permit them to dismiss your uniqueness and attribute characteristics to you that may not be valid or flattering.

What is the older-worker stereotype? According to one survey, it means you don't like anything new and you are physically limited. That's right. The moment you come through the door, many interviewers are going to automatically assume you fit into one or both of these categories before you even open your mouth. What can you do to offset it? First, and most important, you need to acknowledge it may occur. Second, you need to recognize it when it does. And third, you need to know how to offset it with *positive* images during the interview.

Why do interviewers stereotype people? Basically, they are no different from the rest of us. Putting people in preconceived boxes is easier than taking the time to get to know them as individuals. Of course, employers are not the only guilty ones. You do it, too, when you say, "They won't hire

153

someone my age. They're all looking for someone younger."
When they do it to you and you do it to them, no communication occurs.

Prejudice aimed at you

One of your assignments in the interview, then, is to
climb out of the "older worker" box the interviewer may have
put you in and make the person see you as an individual. At
the same time, you should try to see the interviewer as the
unique individual he or she is.

The American Association of Retired Persons (AARP)
funded a survey several years ago to see how American business viewed older reentry workers (defined as 50 years and
older). The research firm of Yankelovich, Skelly and White
conducted on-site interviews with 400 American businesses,
sizes 50 to 1,000-plus employees. In each firm, the person interviewed was either the business owner or the person
directly in charge of human resources or personnel. The survey found that stereotypes, both good and bad, exist concerning older workers.

On the negative side, the survey found that many employers believe older people have physical limitations and
are resistant to new ways. It's imperative, therefore, that you
offset *both* of these stereotypes during each interview. We
once brought up this issue during a workshop, and one
woman said she had recently taken up belly-dancing—
should she mention it during the interview? Absolutely, we
told her. We couldn't think of a better way to negate the
stereotype of being physically limited than the image or her
belly-dancing.

What if you don't do anything as interesting as that? In-
vent something. If you think about it, you can surely uncover
a fact about yourself that will counter the notion that older
people just sit in rocking chairs and watch the world pass by.
Do you swim, jog, bicycle, backpack or play tennis? Any of

these activities will help project the image of the active, vital person you are.

Below list five examples of how active you are that will effectively crush the stereotype of "physical limitation" during your interviews.

1. _____
2. _____
3. _____
4. _____
5. _____

To counter the stereotype that "older people are resistant to new ways," you will need examples of how you welcome change. If you are asked about where you go on vacation, for example, think of what you've done or where you've gone recently that's different. Talk about that backpacking trip you took with your teenage grandson. If you are curious about computers, enroll in a computer class (or say you're thinking about taking a class)—then talk about it during the interview. Don't say you've been going to the same cabin at the same lake for the past 30 years.

List five examples of how you welcome change that you can emphasize during your interviews.

1. _____
2. _____
3. _____
4. _____
5. _____

On the other side of the coin—the plus side—the vast majority of companies in the survey thought older workers were "more knowledgeable than their younger counterparts."

As we all know, just because you're older doesn't necessarily mean you're more knowledgeable. But who says you can't use positive stereotypes to your advantage? So play it up!

Below list five examples of how you're more knowledgeable than your younger counterparts that you can emphasize during your interviews.

1. _____
2. _____
3. _____
4. _____
5. _____

Many companies also attributed a "good work ethic" to older workers. Again, capitalize on this common perception by mentioning that you won't be calling in sick because of boyfriend problems, a sick child, a hangover, etc. Reiterate that your time is your own and you plan to pour both it and your energy into the new job.

Now list five examples of your work ethic that you can emphasize during your interviews.

1. _____
2. _____
3. _____
4. _____
5. _____

Throughout the interview, it's imperative that you accentuate the positive. Human beings, especially interviewers, have selective memories. Say something negative and it will be remembered. (In fact, you will need to make six positive comments to offset every negative comment, so it's easier—and smarter—not to say anything negative at all.)

Now, for your final exercise, look in the mirror. What stereotype might a perspective employer hang on you just by *looking* at you? Below list five examples of what you can do or say to offset the interviewer's unspoken thoughts about your appearance or dress.

1. _____
2. _____
3. _____
4. _____
5. _____

Prejudice your aim at others

Conversely, you need to accept the *interviewer* at face value. This means you should not prejudice yourself about this person before, during or after the interview. If you keep telling yourself there is no way anyone will hire you because you're over 50, you're right, no one will.

Let's examine prejudice for a moment. Where does it come from? How does it form? It has many sources: our childhood, our parents, our culture, our life experiences, our contemporaries. Prejudices form a framework by which we evaluate the world. The tendency to prejudge people will not limit us unduly if we interact only with those who also were raised exactly as we were and if we never venture more than five miles from our birthplace! However, once we attempt to interact with the world at large, we can—and will—run into difficulties. This is because the meanings we learned to attach to particular behaviors may be outdated, obsolete or simply erroneous.

For example, perhaps you would be unnerved if a man interviewing you wore an earring. Based on your notion of how things are (the "information" you have), you might erroneously conclude the interviewer was gay. How you react to

157

these kinds of situations will determine much of what occurs in your interviews. But the real point is that your "information" is outdated; wearing earrings has become a fairly common fashion statement for men under 30 years of age. So you would have allowed your prejudice to cloud and confuse the interview.

Or perhaps you might conclude that a woman executive was bossy because she directed you to take a seat. You may have been raised to believe that men, not women, performed such duties. So you might conclude that this woman would be a difficult boss to work for or will be a tough interviewer and decide to "teach her a thing or two" with a few patronizing remarks during the interview.

The examples could go on and on. How do you know if *you* are guilty of pigeon-holing people? Pay attention to what you mentally conjure up as you meet people. If you attach personality and/or behavioral characteristics to people based solely on what they look like, sound like, dress like, etc., you need to deprogram yourself of prejudicial tendencies. We all fall into patterns and habits, but to succeed in this world (as well as in job search) we must have an open mind. Once we put blinders on, we limit our experiences tremendously. Stay positive and open-minded. If you do, it will come through in both your demeanor and how you present yourself.

Chapter Thirteen

Discouraging Discrimination

Age discrimination, unfortunately, exists. It cuts across economic, cultural and organizational lines and is widespread.

Forcing you out

Exit incentives targeting older workers began in the mid-'70s and continue to the present. Without violating the Age Discrimination in Employment Act (ADEA), "golden parachutes" as this incentive is called, strongly *encourage* older workers to leave "while the going is good."

The facts aren't pretty. Between 1980 and 1990, an estimated 3 million managers, the majority 50-plus, lost their jobs. Three million layoffs translates into roughly one out of four workers. Why wasn't there some sort of public outrage, a congressional investigation—anything? For one thing, the victims are part of a generation that, for the most part, has not learned to fight for its rights.

What motivates these cuts? Are they based solely on age bias? Or are middle managers targeted because, as a group, they are overpaid and underproductive? Certainly the layoffs occur, in part, as a result of organizational survival in a complex and competitive global market. Couldn't a case be made that management's offer of the golden parachute is a benevolent gesture? Many executives think so. In fact, they consider it the most humane way to shrink the managerial work force. Or so said a full one-third of corporate executives polled by the American Management Association a few years back. They indicated they would again offer an exit-incentive package the next time they had to reduce personnel costs. So who are the good guys? Who are the bad guys?

There are several reasons why middle managers (who happen to be 50-plus) were and are often targeted for early retirement or layoffs. First, there's the under-the-surface sentiment that younger people with families should not be laid off. Perhaps this bias is a holdover from one you may have helped perpetuate 25 years ago (the one that said "women have no business taking men's jobs because men have families to support"). And it is true many people in their 50s are in better economic shape; their children are grown and their mortgages are paid.

Second, middle managers make much more than their younger counterparts, usually because of time in service rather than because of greater productivity.

Third, yours is a generation that does what it's told. Frankly, top management thought they could get away with the parachutes and the handshakes. And for the most part, they have.

But you know all this. You may have lived through it yourself. What you may not know is the tide is turning, albeit ever so slowly. And not for any altruistic reason, either. Because of changing demographics. There are now 14 million people over 55 working in America. By the year 2010 the over-55 population will constitute 25 percent of the U.S. work force. Predictions are that when this happens, the older worker will be viewed not as a means to reduce personnel costs, but as the organization's strength. Perhaps there is safety in numbers.

In his book *Age Wave,* Ken Dychtwald examines the importance of these demographics and the continuing impact the Baby Boom generation will have on work, culture, politics, Wall Street, even religion. Unfortunately, the majority of the Boomers will not be in their 50s for another half decade or more. But then, because of the Boomers' numbers, there will be a tremendous change in how the mature worker is viewed by corporate America.

Today we are caught in an awkward transition period—a time when some companies are aggressively recruiting older workers to fill their ranks, while other companies are practicing age discrimination whenever they can get away with it. But if companies are confused, so are many workers. Fifteen years ago, most employees looked forward to retirement and would have gladly bailed out if handed a $75,000 golden parachute and lifetime medical benefits. But times change, values change and people live longer than before. The word is out that early retirement is not all it's cracked up to be. The parachute sometimes crashes, as do marriages and new businesses.

This transition has its share of incongruity and irony. For example, smart companies today are learning how to position themselves for the older consumer of the next decade. Yet some of the very companies that recognize the power of the coming demographics are nonetheless practicing age discrimination in both hiring and firing.

Aren't there laws to protect older workers from this practice? Yes, but it's tough to prove age discrimination. In the last five years especially, employers have learned a lot about what is and what is not considered age discrimination.

Needless to say, they have become more careful and more knowledgeable in protecting themselves from lawsuits.

The ADEA was passed by Congress in 1967. Its original intent was to protect workers age 40 to 65 in the same way Title VII of the Civil Rights Act protects women and minorities in hiring, firing, job placement and promotion. But, unlike the Civil Rights Act, the ADEA holds no provision for affirmative action. Think about that. There is no mandate that older workers be hired first—all things being equal. There are no quotas to fill. Basically, there is no motivation to hire older people. Therefore, my friend, an employer will only hire you if you can solve a problem or meet some need. Bottom line, once again: You'll have to sell yourself.

The ADEA was amended in 1978 to cover people up to age 70 and again in 1986 when Congress eliminated mandatory retirement at any age. As the law currently exists, we never have to retire. Yet in the '80s the average retirement age actually decreased; it currently stands at 62. Of course, much of that early retirement has to do with the golden parachute issue; but in many other cases, workers simply choose early retirement. As much as anything else, it has to do with the power of suggestion.

Once a worker hits 60 or 62 the questions, well-meaning perhaps, start: "So, when are you going to hang 'em up?" "Bet you've been counting the days, huh?" "What are you waiting for?" So you start thinking about it: "Maybe it wouldn't be so bad. Heck, it might even be fun not to have to get up in the morning or fight the commute anymore..." Once you start considering retirement, the issue snowballs, and before you know it, a hard-to-resist exit-incentive package materializes out of nowhere. The gold watch is ordered, the retirement party planned.

Peer pressure, real or imagined, is one thing. But being kicked out is something else again. In their book, *Forced Out: When Veteran Employees Are Driven From Their Careers,* authors Hilda Scott and Juliet Brudney track the experiences of older workers who have been victims of age discrimination. A strong pattern emerges: 10 to 20 years of satisfactory or even exemplary job performance, a change of leadership caused by an economic crunch, then an unsatisfactory performance review. Embarrassed, the employee is stunned into silence. Harassment, subtle and not-so-subtle, begins until the older employee resigns or retires early.

Or the department is reorganized but the same function ends up being handled by another department under another name, with the middle manager being reassigned to a position with little power or purpose. When the employee becomes thoroughly demoralized, he or she is called in and the parachute or "window" is offered. (The package is sometimes called a window because there is a limited time the offer will be "open." If you don't accept it within that time, the opportunity will disappear or "close.") The employee understands clearly that he or she is no longer wanted.

Many who have accepted parachutes have gone forward and started brand-new businesses or careers for themselves. Some even look back on the experience as a blessing in disguise. Others, though, have been so scarred by the experience that they won't even consider reentering the workplace. A 1990 Commonwealth Report indicated there are nearly 2 million retired Americans over 50 who would love to *unretire*. More than half, however, aren't even looking for work. Why?

They're discouraged, they say. Or they're suffering from poor self-esteem. And the only way to build self-esteem is to identify what you want and take the risks necessary to achieve it. If that means girding for battle, so be it.

Scott and Brudney compared the treatment older employees received in nonprofit organizations and social-service agencies with the treatment they got in corporate America. The authors discovered they fared no better in the public sector. Even school districts have their own methods of harassment. One 68-year-old teacher we know was pressured to retire by her administration. Last spring she refused; this fall she was assigned to all the problem classes. She has announced she will retire next semester.

Keeping you out

The ADEA protects all aspects of employment, including hiring. Warning signs of possible age discrimination in the hiring process include any or all of the following:

After expressing an interest in you on the phone, a prospective employer rejects you after an interview because you are "overqualified."

An employer advertises for "recent college graduates" or "people with three to five years experience."

An interviewer asks such questions as "How old are you?" "When do you plan to retire?" "Do you have any health problems?" or "Do you mind working with younger people?"

A younger person with the same or fewer qualifications is hired instead of you.

But remember, an employer's just asking you an age-sensitive question doesn't mean the person won't hire you. He or she may simply be unaware of ADEA regulations and honestly curious about how you would interact with younger people, or whatever.

By now you know the interview is a very subjective evaluation. Rather than expending your energy in the interview trying to catch the employer asking an ageist question or worrying or analyzing why he or she did, pour all your energy into presenting yourself in a positive manner. That way, the interviewer—even if he or she *does* have an age bias—will not be able to group you with all other older people because you will have demonstrated your remarkable uniqueness. Then, after you have the job and are part of the system, you can work to change the age discrimination and stereotyping that exists there.

We suggest this for two reasons. One, it's hard to prove age discrimination in the hiring process. For one thing, it will be almost impossible for you to find out who was hired. You won't have access to that person's resume or application to compare with yours. And the reason given to you for hiring someone else will never be "because he/she is younger." It will be much more difficult to quantify: "better education," "willingness to travel," "better references," etc.

Two, we know you can get a job by enthusiastically presenting yourself to a prospective employer. Perhaps not the first employer or the second or maybe not even the 20th, but somewhere out there is a job matching both your skills and interests. Somewhere out there is an employer anxious to meet you.

Seeking justice

What recourse do you have if you feel you've been discriminated against? For starters, you must file a complaint with the proper federal or state agency within 180 days of the discriminating event. In 1979 the responsibility for enforcement of the ADEA transferred from the Labor Department to the Equal Employment Opportunity Commission (EEOC). In addition to the EEOC, each state can have its own age-discrimination laws and an agency to back them up.

Phone your local or regional EEOC to determine the best method for filing your complaint. Either your state agency or the EEOC can investigate on your behalf and will determine "probable cause for crediting the allegations" or "lack of probable cause." If the finding is "probable cause," the agency will hold a face-to-face conference with you and the employer and attempt to reconcile the matter first.

If reconciliation fails, you may want to take the claim to court. While the state or federal agency can represent you in court, those profiled in *Forced Out* were disappointed with the legal advice they received. So you may want to hire your own lawyer. If the suit is class-action, you stand a better chance of winning. Jury-ordered remedies have, to date, included reinstatement, back pay (wages lost up to judgment), front pay (prospective wages in lieu of reinstatement), and attorney's fees and costs.

But often it's not enough to simply feel you've been wronged. There are all sorts of "wrongs" in our society. The law does not guarantee "fairness," but only protection against unlawful behaviors. For you to win a case, age must be the determining factor. The fact that management cleaned house (you, at age 55, being among those who were swept out) or that you had a personality conflict with your boss who blocked your advancement is not sufficient to establish a case for age discrimination.

Eugene Goodman, an international marketing executive, won a case against his employer after he was passed over four times in favor of younger men when he had been promised a vice presidency. It took him six years and his life savings, but he was awarded more than $450,000 by the jury. In 1983 he published his litigation experience in *All the Justice I Could Afford*.

More recently, Elizabeth Layman, a former software marketing specialist for Xerox Corporation, sued the firm charging age discrimination. In 1986, when she was 43 years old, she agreed, at company request, to transfer to California in a comparable position. She made her plans and sold her home. At the last minute she discovered the transfer was to an entry-level job at a substantial pay cut, and she declined it. Her position in Dallas was later filled by a man seven years younger than she. The case took four years in court, but when she won, she won handsomely—she was awarded $8.75 million in punitive damages, $145,000 in back pay and lost benefits, and nearly $140,000 in compensatory damages.

(Ironically, Xerox is one of several major companies that have been heralded for innovative phased-retirement programs.)

If called in by the EEOC, your employer may attempt to modify and/or falsify your evaluations, so document everything: memos, meetings, written offers, copies of all evaluations and reviews, notes of any comments that indicate a culture or environment that promotes age discrimination, etc. You'll need it because it's a case of David versus Goliath—and guess who's David?

Looking forward

But there is good news. For every person or firm that practices age discrimination, 10 others don't. In fact, there are companies and industries that specifically recruit older workers.

Nearly 14 million new service jobs were created between 1970 and 1988 and many of these employers are clamoring for older workers. Hardware stores and home-improvement chains like Builders Emporium recruit over-55 employees; a more mature face makes more sense in such retail environments. And temporary agencies have discovered the benefits of placing older workers as well; seniors now make up one-fourth of Manpower's work force. Adia has just debuted a recruitment video aimed at older reentry workers. When Kelly Services began actively recruiting retirees in 1987, 7 percent of its 550,000 temporary employees were 55 or older; by 1989 that proportion had grown to 12 percent.

Days Inn has instructed its job recruiters to go after men and women over 50. Walt Disney actively recruits retirees to fill vacancies on its 25,000 Disney World staff. Tourism and travel is the fastest-growing business in the U.S. today, and by the end of the next decade it will employ one out of five American workers. Because one in four pleasure trips is taken by the 55-plus traveler, these industries are aggressively seeking older employees.

Did you know Travelers Corporation runs a Retiree Job Bank that fills 60 percent of its company's temporary employment needs? It was first organized in 1981 and today has an active pool of 750 retirees; one-half are retired Travelers employees, the other half are not. Travelers has even changed its pension plan so retired people can work up to 960 hours without losing their benefits.

Banks are hiring retired workers as tellers and customer-service representatives. Bank of America in Los Angeles hired 300 people over age 60 in 1988 and another 400 in the first half of 1989.

AARP runs a computerized National Older Worker Information System that documents the "good guys." To date, more than 369 companies are listed in its file. All of these firms provide innovative options for older workers including employment pools, phased retirement, training programs, etc.

So a few businesses want to hire you because of how old you are; but many more want to hire you because of who you are. Look around at all the role models you see being recognized for their achievements. In 1988 Frances Lear (age 62) launched *Lear's* for the over-40 woman. Today the magazine is going strong and the editorials, articles, interviews and fashions are for mature women in charge of their lives. Lear's motivation in starting the magazine was that she was fed up with the youth-driven *Cosmopolitans* and *Vogues*. *Lear's* fit the bill.

Middle-aged and older actors and entertainers have made strong comebacks in the last few years—and not as doddering character actors but as leading men and women. In 1989 Sean Connery (age 59) was named "Sexiest Man of the Year" by *People* magazine. Paul Newman still twinkles his baby blues in his 60s; Frank Sinatra still does it his way at 75-plus, and Johnny Carson, though now retired, continues to be considered the best late night host.

Mary Kay is hailed as a true entrepreneur; Sophia Loren and Elizabeth Taylor continue to fascinate the public; and Margaret Thatcher's strong politics helped change the United Kingdom forever.

In your city and community there are older people working and succeeding and accomplishing in all fields and at all endeavors. And if you asked them, they would all have this in common: They aren't conscious of being older. They just like doing what they're doing and it never occurs to them that they can't do it. Now it's your turn!

Chapter Fourteen

Acing the Interview

Here it is. The moment has come. It's make or break time. The interview is your chance to demonstrate everything you now know about job search. You'll do beautifully. You know everything you need to know to pull off a great interview and get that job offer. The end is in sight.

In fact, you can afford to relax a little bit. That's because if the employer wasn't interested, you would not have been called in for the interview. He or she knows you've got what it takes for the job. The interview is really only a personality and image test. And now you know how to make both of those work for you.

View the interview as a win-win situation. Yes, the prospective employer is checking you out, trying to decide if you are someone he or she wants to work with on a daily basis, and trying to assess whether you will enhance his or her position and image, as well as that of the organization. But, on the other hand, you should assess the employer, too. Is this someone you would like to work for? Do you like what you hear about the organization? Is it a good match for you?

The interview is hard work, make no mistake about it, but it also can be a fun and exhilarating experience if you handle it well. Since you clearly don't have the job before the interview, *you really have nothing to lose.* If you don't get the job—well, it wasn't yours anyway (that should be a liberating thought). When you think about it, the interviewer has only as much power over you as you choose to give him or her.

From your side of the interview, you will need to communicate all of your plus factors. Let the employer get to know you—and like you. It is important to come across as being as professional as the person facing you. Therefore, dress as well as (if not better than) the interviewer. Bring your resume (in case the one you sent has been misplaced) and be well-versed on all of its parts.

Be sure your answers to the interviewer's questions are clear, credible and consistent. No hedging, no inconsistencies. Think out the logic of your responses and practice them. Not once, not twice, but many times. Emphasize the positive aspects of your age—work ethic, loyalty, good health, high energy, enthusiasm, maturity, flexibility, etc. Be aware of the not-so-great stereotypes that exist about older workers and make sure your answers offset them. The interviewer will invariably ask some questions that will cause you some anxiety. This standard interview technique is used for two reasons: 1) The interviewer wants to see how you handle pressure; and 2) if you are hiding something, she hopes her questions will unnerve you so you'll divulge something you weren't planning to.

Expect the standard "Tell me about yourself" request (see Question 10 on page 177 for further explanation). Plan for it, rehearse it, and deliver a summary of your work experience and current situation in the most upbeat terms possible. No matter how much you need the job, *do not show it.* How much you need the job is not relevant to the interviewer; in fact, it will work against you. Instead, project the image of someone who is researching different companies and different situations to find the best possible match.

When the interviewer asks if you have any questions, the answer is always *yes*. But don't ask questions about work benefits (vacation days, dental plan, etc.). Believe it or not, the interviewer has forgotten he or she works for money at this point and believes he or she works for "personal satisfaction" or as part of an exciting team that is "getting something done." Therefore, act like you are similarly motivated and share those concerns. Researching the firm beforehand will help you generate questions to ask or topics to bring up. Good topics to ask about are expansion plans, major competitors, corporate image, etc. Nothing too personal.

The 10 most often-asked questions

The following questions may also be asked of you. Included is an ideal response for each one, and a short rationale following it. Practice each answer until you are comfortable with it. Listen carefully to each question asked of you before responding. If you miss part of a question or don't understand it, *don't attempt to answer*. Rather, smile and ask for clarification.

You may be lucky. You might be the type of person who interviews once and is hired immediately. Or you might be the kind of person who goes on 20 interviews before a good match is struck. It's the luck of the draw.

1. "What are your ideas on salary?"
"It's negotiable. But first, let's see if I'm someone you'd like to hire and if this is a place I'd like to work. Then I'll be happy to discuss salary."

Avoid mentioning a salary figure here because, in all probability, your figure will be too high or too low. If it's too high and this is the first interview, you'll be screened out. If it's too low, the interviewer may think (stereotype) you're not qualified and you'll be screened out. Eventually, after your second or third interview, you will want to—and have to—discuss money. When that happens, try to get the employer to throw out the first figure. That way you will have a starting place from which to negotiate. The other reason not to talk money up front is because it's to your advantage to act as though you are exploring satisfying career options—not grubbing after money. That is especially true if your primary reason for going to work is money!

2. "Why would you like to work for our company?"
"I've done quite a bit of research. I've interviewed people in this industry, and the message I keep getting is that your company is one of the best. I want to associate with a winner."

If you know something specific and favorable about this firm, now is the time to interject it. This shows you are serious about pursuing a real career opportunity and not just responding to every want-ad you see.

3. "Why have you been unemployed all this time?"
"I've been really fortunate to have some time off. It's given me the chance to do some serious soul-searching, and I've decided I'm _____."

Whatever your response is here, start with a positive beginning and wrap it up with a positive ending. Turn the experience into something that could be beneficial to the employer.

4. "How long do you expect to work here?"
"As long as it's mutually beneficial."

This question seems to be asked more of older workers than of younger ones. An employer has two fears about your work future. One is that the company may not be able to get rid of you—even when it *is* time for you to retire. The other is that the company will spend time and money training you, you'll get sick and quit, and this whole search/application/ interview process will have to be repeated. The answer here indicates that when it's appropriate for you to retire, you will. It also suggests that you view yourself as in control of your life: If or when the work no longer holds meaning for you, you will look elsewhere because how you spend your time and energy matter to you.

5. "Do you have or have you had any serious illness or injury?"

"I'm glad you asked that. I'm in terrific health and intend to stay that way."

One of prospective employers' major concerns is that older employees get sick easier and stay sick longer. The employer does not really want to know about your hernia or gall-bladder operation—so don't mention them. Again, you want to give positive, upbeat answers. just answering "No" is not sufficient; besides, it sounds evasive. Round out your responses with examples.

6. "How would you feel about working for a younger manager?"

"Great. I respect competence at any age."

Obviously, you cannot say you can't or don't want to work for someone younger than you—even if it's true. This response works nicely because it shows you are cooperative, are in charge, and have a sense of humor.

7. "What do you do in your spare time?"

"I bought myself a computer two months ago and have been spending lots of time learning how to operate it. I'm actually getting pretty good at it."

or

"I'm very active in my church and in community affairs. People keep volunteering me to be in charge of this or that fund raiser. I do it because I'm good at it and love it."

or

"My grandkids live nearby and I take them on excursions as often as I can. We bounce all over. It's great fun."

This question gives you an opportunity to dispel the stereotype that "older people are resistant to change." So provide a lively example or two that shows you to be an inquiring, capable, active individual.

8. "We have many qualified applicants. Why should we hire you?"

"I don't know about your other applicants, but I do know about myself. I am a quick learner, have lots of energy, and care tremendously about the quality of work I produce."

You can also insert something about your experience and skills, but always *stress the future* rather than past accomplishments. Remember, the interviewer already knows you're qualified to do the job. Think and talk benefits.

9. "What are your strengths and weaknesses?"

"My strengths are I listen well, have excellent follow-through, am a quick learner, etc." (Fill in your own list of strengths below.)

1. _____
2. _____
3. _____
4. _____
5. _____

"My weaknesses are chocolate-chip cookies, Ella Fitzgerald, and golf—anytime, anywhere!" (Fill in your own clever responses on the next page.)

1. _____
2. _____
3. _____
4. _____
5. _____

Obviously, the goal here is to accentuate the positive as much as possible when talking about strengths and to avoid the negative when discussing weaknesses. Don't literally provide a list of the weaknesses you're working on. Honesty has its place, but not here.

10. "Tell me about yourself."

"I guess you could call me a reentry homemaker. I raised my children and managed my home for 25 years. Now the children are out and doing well, and I feel good about that accomplishment. Now it's time for me. While I was home I did quite a bit of volunteer work and became skilled at fund-raising. I've chaired fund-raising committees for the PTA, the American Cancer Society and the Junior League. I've become a good public speaker and know this talent, combined with my fund-raising abilities and organizational skills, gives me all the attributes I need to be successful in this field."

or

"I'm one of those fellows you always hear about. You know, the one who plans his retirement to a 'T.' Except I forgot to take one important variable into account: I thrive on people and projects. And to be honest, since I've been home the past six months, I've been bored. Oh, I've tried travel, new hobbies, volunteering, you name it. It just isn't me. I like producing; I guess I miss the deadlines. So I'm returning to work."

or

"I worked for XYZ Corporation for 20 years as a _____. When it merged with ABC last year I was presented with several options. The one I chose was early retirement. This last year, I've had the luxury of figuring out what I want to do with the rest of my career life. I've done a lot of self-analysis and have concluded I want a position where I can train other _____. I'm interviewing with half a dozen similar organizations and have learned a lot in the interviews. It's a pretty exciting time for me."

This is one of those great innocuous questions that will be asked during your interview. What do they want to know? For starters, let's discuss what they *don't* want to know. They don't want to know where you were born, how many children you have, or what you do with your spare time—or anything too confusing or irrelevant. What you want to do is make the interview as simple for the employer as possible. Summarize the last five years or so of your life in upbeat terms and calmly explain why you are interested in returning to work. In the space below, try your own response to this question. Practice it in front of the mirror 20 times until you are calm and convincing.

_____

_____

_____

_____

_____

_____

_____

_____

_____

_____

_____

_____

Now re-read what you wrote. Is it upbeat? Is it concise? Is it interesting? Is it relevant? Will the interviewer quickly get a handle on who you are? Remember stereotyping. Give the interviewer an answer that allows him or her to put you in a positively labeled box: reentry housewife, retired person who is too active to remain at home, someone in a mid-life career change, etc. If you need to, rewrite your response.

_____

_____

_____

_____

_____

_____

_____

_____

_____

_____

_____

_____

_____

Before you leave

Most interviews conclude with the interviewer saying something like, "Thanks for coming in. I have several more candidates to interview before I make my decision. But I should have an answer for you by Thursday. We'll get in touch with you." If you've noticed, there has been a real shift of power here: The interviewer now has all of it. But don't worry, you still have a few more aces up your sleeve.

You can't just lie down and give this person all this power over you. It's not psychologically healthy. Therefore, it is imperative that you say, "Great. I look forward to hearing from you. But, you know, I'm in and out a great deal right now on interviews and such. If I don't hear from you by Thursday afternoon, would you mind if I called you first thing Friday morning?"

The interviewer can't possibly object, having already said he or she will call you on the preceding day. By doing this, you not only will feel you have more control, you will be in control.

On the practical side, you don't have to wait by the phone until Thursday and you can actively pursue other jobs. The interviewer will sense a shift of power and, if you do it subtlety, will acknowledge it gracefully. Remember, hiring is an emotional decision, and you want to come across as powerfully as you can—without intimidating the interviewer.

Following up

We have a favorite saying: *Everything takes longer than it takes.* This is especially true in business—and hiring. When interviewers say you will hear from them by Thursday, they probably believe that to be the case. They don't yet know a crisis will develop late Monday afternoon that will take all of their time and wits and that they'll have to postpone the rest of the interviews until Friday. This is much more likely to happen than not. Therefore, it's mandatory that you call the interviewer Friday morning *as you said you would.*

What do you say? Identify yourself and ask if the decision has been made. Don't *point out that the interviewer didn't call you on Thursday as promised—he or she knows that!*

Calling interviewers back is a good move on four accounts.

First, it brings you back into their thoughts, forcing them to reevaluate you. Second, it shows you can be assertive without being abrasive. Third, it shows you are interested in the position. Fourth, it proves your follow-through is good.

What happens if you are told someone else was selected? Naturally, your feelings are hurt and you just want to get off the phone and lick your wounds in peace. Don't! Now is the time to be tough. Take a deep breath and say, "Well, I'm sorry you didn't select me. I know I would have been great as your _____. But that's OK. You know I'm a little new at this interviewing business, so can you tell me what I could have said or done differently to have been your top candidate?" Practice this many times before you attempt it for real. Work at keeping your voice calm and unchallenging. Try to use the same tone of voice you would use if you were asking someone to pass the salt.

Why should you go through this agonizing exercise? For starters, you may find out something about your interviewing style that has been holding you back. You may learn you didn't know something technical about the job in question. You may discover the decision had nothing to do with you at all—the company may have been simply going through the motions because management had already selected someone from the inside.

But the most important reason for asking is that sometimes the selected candidate doesn't work out. If you make an effort to bolster your relationship with the employer, however, chances are good you'll be asked to come back for another interview. After all, how many unchosen candidates would think of doing this? If you don't make the gesture, you'll probably never be asked back—especially if you got a form letter saying you weren't hired and you do nothing about it.

Most interviewers are not ogres. They know you want the job and they don't like hurting people's feelings any more than you do. Therefore, they'll just avoid you. But, if you basically tell them, "Hey, it's OK that you made the choice you did; no hard feelings," you stand a much better chance of being called back. It's just human nature.

One more thing: Practice. Practice. Practice. Select someone whose opinion you respect and ask that person to role-play the interview with you. By the second run-through, this "interviewer" will start to take his or her role seriously, and that's when you should ask for feedback: Which of your responses sound natural? Which need more work? Remind the person that all your answers should be positive and to tell you when they aren't. You'll both know when you're ready: You'll begin to enjoy the exercise, you'll start to joke about it, and most importantly, you'll present yourself convincingly and comfortably. And then your role-play interviewer will have no choice but to offer you the job!

You Did It!

You worked your way through the self-assessment exercises, the risk-taking, the informational interviews, and a role-played interview. Congratulations! If you are not already employed, you soon will be. Although entitled *Finding a Job After 50*, this book could just as easily have been titled *Self-Empowerment Through Self-Advocacy*.

We firmly believe personal power is synonymous with our view of ourselves and our level of self-understanding. Yet, if it's a matter of what comes first, I'd have to say that self-understanding is precursory to self-empowerment. This has been the guiding logic of *Finding a Job After 50*.

Over the years we've come to realize that people cannot and will not take appropriate risks unless they have a good understanding of their own realized and unrealized potentials. That is why *Finding a Job After 50* begins with the issues of personal growth and the power of risk-taking. That is also why the book is laced with self-assessment/self-understanding exercises. Everyone begins job search at a different place. In *Finding a Job After 50* we provide you with a structure by which you have developed your own job-search roadmap.

As you have learned, the process of self-understanding does not come in a jar or even in a book. Sometimes the inward search seems to move at the slowest possible pace; but at other times, the sudden comprehension of relationships and self-understanding comes so quickly it takes your breath away. *Finding a Job After 50* has led you through the process of self-assessment. Through the process of self-examination you'll arrive at self-understanding and, ultimately, self-acceptance.

With understanding and acceptance come personal power. Because there are no games to play, because the facade is gone, you are just who you are. It is at this point, when personal power emerges, that you begin to take some risks. With risk comes potential reward—as in a job that matches and meshes with who you are today.

You are employable. There are many employers out there who would be delighted to hire you, with all your skills, abilities and life experience, except they don't know who you are. It's up to you to find them and tell them. Now that you understand the potential payoffs to risk and you possess the tools for creative job search, you will be able to quickly identify those employers. And best of all, you now have a much stronger understanding of what you want from a job as well as from your life.

Finally, job search is hard work, and it can and will wear you down. Choose your mate or an empathetic friend—someone you trust—to share the ups and downs of this journey. Explain that you need a cheerleader, someone on your side, and ask point-blank if this confidant is up to the job. If the person hesitates, find someone else. Then share each interview experience, both the good and the not-so-good. Lean on your cheerleader when times are tough; celebrate with him or her when the light breaks through.

These exercises and concepts have propelled hundreds of reentry people into satisfying careers. It will work for you, too. Just trust in what you've learned and let loose. Good luck, and keep that sparkle in your eye. It makes people wonder what you've been up to!

Appendix

General reading

How to Promote Your Own Business, Gary Blake and Robert W. Bly, New York: The New American Library, 1983

Forced Out: When Veteran Employees Are Driven From Their Careers, Juliet Brudney and Hilda Scott, New York: Simon and Schuster, 1987

The Seven Habits of Highly Effective People: Restoring the Character Ethic, Steven R. Covey, New York: Simon & Schuster, 1989

Age Wave, Ken Dychtwald, Los Angeles: Jeremy Tarcher, Inc., 1989

Your Erroneous Zones, Dr. Wayne Dyer, New York: Avon Books, 1976

Guerrilla Marketing Attack, Jay Conrad Levinson, Boston: Houghton Mifflin Company, 1989

Success Over Sixty, Albert Myers and Christopher P. Andersen, New York: Summit Books, 1984

Enough Is Enough, Carol Orsborn, New York: G.P. Putnam's Sons, 1986

In Search of Excellence, Thomas Peters and Robert Waterman, Jr., New York: Harper and Row, 1982

Passages, Gail Sheehy, New York: Bantam Books, 1976

Necessary Losses, Judith Viorst, New York: Ballantine Books, 1986

How-to career books

Finding the Right Job at Midlife, Jeffrey Allen, New York: Simon & Schuster, 1985

What Color Is Your Parachute? A Practical Manual for Job-Hunters and Career-Changers, Richard Nelson Bolles, Berkeley, California: Ten Speed Press, 1991

Resume and Job-Hunting Guide for Present and Future Veterans, Caroline Steed De Prez, New York: Arco Books, 1984

Ready, *Aim, You're Hired: How to Job-Interview Successfully Anytime, Anywhere with Anyone,* Paul Hellman, New York: American Management Association, 1986

Pack Your Own Parachute: How to Survive Mergers, Takeovers and Other Corporate Disasters, Paul Morris Hirsch, Reading, Massachusetts: Addison-Wesley, 1987

Job Search Manual for Mature Workers, Fred Merrill, Los Angeles Council on Careers for Older Americans, 5225 Wilshire Blvd., Ste. 204, Los Angeles, CA 90036; 213-939-0391.

Knock 'Em Dead: With Great Answers to Tough Interview Questions, Martin John Yate, Boston: B. Adams, 1985

The Smart Woman's Guide to Resumes and Job Hunting, Julie Adair King and Betsy Sheldon, New Jersey: Career Press, 1993

Take This Job and Leave It, Bill Radin, New Jersey: Career Press, 1992

Part-Time Careers, Joyce Hadley, New Jersey: Career Press, 1993

Reference materials

The Professional and Trade Association Job Finder: A Directory of Employment Resources Offered by Associations and Other Organizations, S. Norman Feingold and Avis Nicholson, Garret Park, Maryland: Garret Park Press, 1985

The Jobs Rated Almanac, Les Kranz, New York: Pharos, 1988

Occupational Outlook Handbook, Washington, D.C.: USGPO, 1988

The American Almanac of Jobs and Salaries, John W. Wright, New York: Avon, 1987

The Job Bank Series: Available each year on the following: Atlanta, Boston, Chicago, Dallas, Denver, Detroit, Florida, Houston, Los Angeles, Minneapolis, New York, Ohio, Phoenix, Philadelphia, San Francisco, St. Louis, Seattle, and Washington, D.C. Holbrook, Massachusetts: Bob Adams, Inc. To order by phone, call 617-767-8100.

Organizations

The National Council on the Aging, Inc.
600 Maryland Avenue SW
West Wing 100
Washington, DC 20024
202-479-1200

The National Caucus and Center on Black Aged, Inc.
1424 K Street NW—Suite 500
Washington, DC 20005
202-637-8400

National Council of Senior Citizens/Sr. Aides Program
925 15th Street NW
Washington, DC 20005
202-347-8800

American Association of Retired Persons (National Older Workers Information System (NOWIS)
1909 K Street NW
Washington, DC 20049
202-872-4700

Gray Panthers
1424 16th St. NW—Ste. 602
Washington, DC 20036
202-387-3111

Gerontological Society of America
1275 K Street NW—Suite 350
Washington, DC 20005
202-543-7446

Older Women's League
730 11th Street NW
Washington, DC 20001
202-783-6686

Forty-Plus (National Office)
1718 P Street NW—Suite T-4
Washington, DC 20036
202-387-1582

Office of National Programs for Older Workers (U.S. Department of Labor, Employment & Training Administration)
200 Constitution Avenue
Frances Perkins Bldg., Ste. 4649
Washington, DC 21210
202-535-0521

Equal Employment Opportunity Commission
1801 L Street NW
Washington, DC 20507
202-663-4264

Senior Career Planning & Placement Service
257 Park Avenue So.
New York, NY 10010
212-529-6660

Operation ABLE
180 N. Wabash Ave.—Ste. 802
Chicago, IL 60601
312-782-3335

About the Authors

Karen and Terry Harty have been actively involved in employment and training issues and outplacement services for over 15 years. In 1983 they formed "The Marketing Concern," a training and consulting firm. The ideas and strategies in *Finding a Job After 50* are the culmination of their highly successful "Back to Work" motivational seminars and the in-depth job-search programs they developed for both corporations and public groups.

Karen and Terry reside in the San Francisco Bay area and together have six children: Talbot, Tanya, Patrick, Julie, Katie and Stephanie.

Index